VENEZUELA

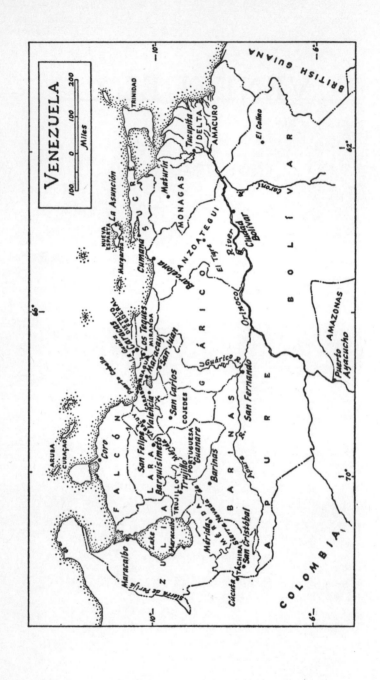

VENEZUELA

by
EDWIN LIEUWEN

SECOND EDITION

Issued under the auspices of the
Royal Institute of International Affairs

OXFORD UNIVERSITY PRESS
LONDON NEW YORK TORONTO
1965

Oxford University Press, Amen House, London E.C.4

GLASGOW   NEW YORK   TORONTO   MELBOURNE   WELLINGTON
BOMBAY   CALCUTTA   MADRAS   KARACHI   LAHORE   DACCA
CAPE TOWN   SALISBURY   NAIROBI   IBADAN   ACCRA
KUALA LUMPUR   HONG KONG

© Royal Institute of International Affairs, 1961, 1965

First published 1961
Second Edition 1965

PRINTED IN GREAT BRITAIN

PREFACE

I LIVED in Caracas in 1950 and 1951, during which time I had an opportunity to visit all twenty states, all the major cities, and every oilfield and refinery. One by-product of this sojourn was my book *Petroleum in Venezuela*, published by the University of California Press in 1954. I visited Venezuela again during 1956. Over the past decade I have had good opportunities to follow closely the extraordinarily rapid political, social, and economic changes that have characterized Venezuela's recent history, either from my United States government posts dealing with Latin American affairs (1952-3, 1955-7) or from my academic employment as Professor of Modern Latin American History (1953-5, and 1957 to the present time). I also keep up a steady correspondence with my many good Venezuelan friends.

Particularly because of the dynamic quality of her modern history, Venezuela is an extremely fascinating country to study. Many revolutionary developments are so recent that it is too early to see them in proper perspective. Consequently I make no pretence that my assessment of Venezuela is in any way definitive. It is my opinion that the key to understanding contemporary Venezuela is to appreciate the inexorable, but for the most part non-violent, social revolution that has been sweeping that nation since the end of the Second World War. In this process the class structure is being altered; wealth and property are being redistributed; the economy is being transformed; institutions are undergoing drastic changes, and political processes have come under the control, for the first time, of genuine reform elements.

In many respects Venezuela's reformers have set an example which revolutionary leaders elsewhere might well be advised to follow. For her leaders have generally tried to steer the country through its 'revolution of rising expecta-

vii

Preface

tions' by moderating the extremes of nationalism characteristic elsewhere and by eschewing the methods of violence,
force, and demagoguery. It is especially promising that they
continue to hold uncompromisingly to the democratic path
even in the face of the 1948–57 decade of dictatorial coun-
ter-revolution and reaction.

For bringing this volume to completion I am indebted to
the University of New Mexico in Albuquerque for a summer research grant, to the Banco Central in Caracas for
statistical information, and to the Venezuelan Information
Service in Washington for a broad variety of miscellaneous
materials.

E. L.

Albuquerque, New Mexico
January 1961

CONTENTS

PRINCIPAL ABBREVIATIONS

AD	Democratic Action
ARS	A dissident AD group
COPEI	Independent Committee for Political and Electoral Organization
FDP	People's Democratic Force
FEI	Independent Electoral Front
IPFN	Independent National Front
MIR	Movement of the Revolutionary Left
ORVE	Venezuelan Organization
PCV	Venezuelan Communist Party
PDN	Democratic National Party
PDV	Venezuelan Democratic Party
UP	Popular Union
UPM	Patriotic Military Union
URD	Republican Democratic Union
VBEC	Venezuelan Basic Economic Corporation
VDC	Venezuelan Development Corporation

Chapter I

THE LAND AND THE PEOPLE

VENEZUELA lies on the north coast of South America. Its narrow southern foot almost touches the Equator while its broad northern face is washed by the Caribbean sea. It is bounded on the west, south, and east by Colombia, Brazil, and British Guiana. Its 352,150 square miles of territory make it the seventh largest country in Latin America.

PHYSIOGRAPHY

At one time the land area of present-day Venezuela was a part of the Guayana land mass, the north-western extension of the ancient continent of Gondwana. The mainland probably extended beyond the present Caribbean coast, but after many ages of geological change and disturbance, the only exposed part of the ancient land mass is the Guayana highlands, the mountainous southern half of the republic which slopes northward to the Orinoco, where it is covered by later formations. After the Guayana highlands were shaped and while new formations from the Caribbean were forcing themselves upward, the Andes began to form. The Venezuelan spur of this great young mountain chain bifurcates upon entering the south-western part of the country. Its left branch, the Sierra de Perijá, strikes directly northward to the sea, while its right branch, forming the Venezuelan Andes, runs in a north-westerly direction till it nears the Caribbean, and then travels parallel to the shore. Thus Venezuela, geologically speaking, is simply a broad alluvial basin bounded by two great mountain systems, the most northerly of which slopes sharply down into a narrow coastal plain.

Ever since man first appeared, the physical features of the Venezuelan landscape have exerted determining influence upon the pattern of settlement and economic activity. In the twentieth century, with the discovery and large-scale exploitation of rich natural resources, Venezuela's geological history has taken on a new and important meaning. For in the two synclines between the mountains—between the Sierra de Perijá and the Andes and between the Andes and the Guayana highlands—the multiple layers of sedimentary rock have been oozing forth petroleum in such ever-increasing quantities that Venezuela for the past quarter century has been the leading exporter and second producer of oil in the world. And recently, in the igneous rock structure of the Guayana highlands, high-grade iron-ore deposits, believed to be the largest in the world, have been discovered.

The accidents of geological history have not only made Venezuela a nation of great natural wealth, but have also divided it into four distinct geographical entities—the coastal lowlands, the Andes, the intermontane plains or *llanos*, and the Guayana highlands—each differing markedly in its physical and cultural characteristics.[1]

THE COASTAL ZONE

The smallest and most northerly of these four major geographical zones is the coastal lowland between the Andes and the Caribbean sea. It includes only 7 per cent. of the republic's area, even counting the seventy adjacent small islands and the Island of Margarita. It is extremely narrow at the centre but broadens appreciably at both ends forming the Orinoco delta at its eastern extremity and the Maracaibo basin in the west.

The whole coastal zone is hot. It has an annual average temperature of over 80° F. High humidity, except in the Paraguaná and Punta de Araya peninsular regions, renders the climate still more oppressive. Yet fully 18 per cent. of the population lives here.

In the narrow central zone lie the ports of La Guaira and

[1] See accompanying map.

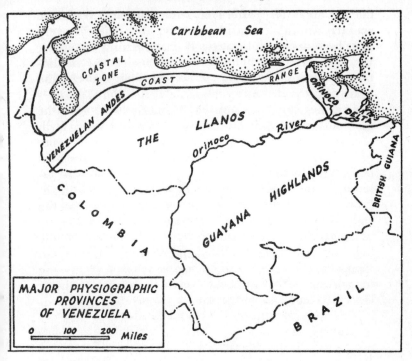

MAJOR PHYSIOGRAPHIC
PROVINCES
OF VENEZUELA

0   100   200 Miles

Puerto Cabello, which handle the great bulk of the nation's agricultural exports and its manufactured imports and thus serve the central population nucleus in the adjacent mountain region. On this central coastal strip are cacao and banana plantations, fisheries, and beach resorts.

The outlying broad coastal zones are closely tied to foreign industry. Maracaibo (Venezuela's second city), Amuay, and Punta Cardón in the west are petroleum ports, while in the east Puerto la Cruz on the Caribbean and Puerto Ordaz near the mouth of the Orinoco serve respectively the oil and iron industries of the interior.

From the Maracaibo basin, which roughly coincides with the boundaries of the state of Zulia, comes two-thirds of the nation's oil. Within the great V formed by the Sierra de Perijá and the Venezuelan Andes, the sediments that have been deposited throughout the ages—in some places they are over three miles deep—are effectively sealed on the mountain sides by non-porous rocks and on the Caribbean side by an impervious anticlinal formation. It is these geological conditions that have proved ideal for the accumulation of such vast quantities of petroleum.

In the centre of this basin, and comprising about one-fifth of its area, is Lake Maracaibo. This shallow, oblong body of nearly fresh water drains the rivers of the adjacent lowlands and empties into the Caribbean, providing natural transportation for the entire region. At its southern end, heavy rainfall and mountain springs make the vegetation dense, the streams numerous, and the climate humid. Subsistence farming and fishing go on here. The northern shore of the lake is much dryer, mainly because the prevailing north-easterly Caribbean breezes do not pass over surfaces sufficiently high to produce condensation.

This same low altitude factor and the absence of near-by mountains have produced Venezuela's only desert just north-east of the Maracaibo basin on the Paraguaná Peninsula. In this sparsely inhabited area the land is quite useless for agriculture. There is some fishing and goat raising here, but oil refining is the main form of economic activity on the peninsula.

The eastern coastal zone displays roughly the same climatic picture as the west. The broad Orinoco delta region, virtually uninhabited except for scattered primitive Indian groups, is made an area of very high precipitation and tropical jungle vegetation by the clash of contrary winds. Farther north, on the Caribbean coast and the adjacent islands, the coastal lowlands are quite dry. Oil refining and shipping at Puerto la Cruz, salt works at Punta de Araya, pearl fishing and tourist industries on Margarita Island, and commercial fishing off Cumaná and Barcelona are the principal forms of economic activity here.

THE ANDES

The northern mountain region is the core of the nation. In this geographical zone, which comprises only 12 per cent. of the land area, 70 per cent. of the people live. The density of population here is related to the pleasantness of the climate, which is rendered moderate by altitude. The annual mean temperature in the major cities of this region ranges from 61°F. at Mérida to 77° at Barquisimeto and Valencia. In Caracas, the capital, it is 70°.

Venezuela's highest mountains are the 300-mile-long Sierra Nevada de Mérida range, which forms the right wing of the V making up the Maracaibo basin. It has many peaks above the snow line (15,400 ft.), topped by the Pico Bolívar (16,411 ft.). In the foothills the climate and vegetation remain tropical up to 3,000 feet. This is the Tierra Caliente zone. It is in the intermontane valleys of the moderate Tierra Templada zone (3,000–6,000 ft.) that settlement is concentrated. Here are located the important cities of San Cristóbal, Mérida, Valera, and Trujillo, and here on the mountain sides is cultivated most of Venezuela's coffee, the chief export crop. In the Tierra Fría (above 6,000 ft.) wheat and potatoes are grown.

The Sierra Nevada runs into the coast range, a mountain system of similar length and breadth but lesser elevation, the crest here reaching only 7,000–9,000 feet. In the western half of the coast range coffee and maize are produced, and cattle are raised. At Barquisimeto, the republic's third largest city, there is a growing amount of industrial activity.

The central portion of the coast range, the region around Caracas, is the hub of Venezuela. The capital city itself has over a million inhabitants and is the nation's commercial and industrial centre as well as the seat of government. Caracas and important neighbouring cities such as Valencia, the nation's agricultural metropolis, and Maracay, the centre of the cattle industry, are situated in the warm, fertile valleys between the crest of the coast range and an interior ridge to the south. From the Valencia basin the rich soil around Lake Valencia produces the greater part of Venezuela's sugar cane, cotton, rice, and citrus fruit. At Maracay the scrubby cattle from the interior plains are fattened in the surrounding green pastures, then slaughtered, and the meat is then marketed in the major cities of the republic.

The easternmost extension of the Andes forms the highlands behind the coastal cities of Barcelona and Cumaná. The mountains here drop to less than 3,000 feet, so that the climate is more tropical than temperate. Subsistence agriculture is the main economic activity, though some cacao is grown on the mountain sides.

Finally, in the Venezuelan Andes system, there is the Sierra de Perijá at the far western edge of the republic. This range is of little importance in the effective politics, economy, and society of Venezuela, for in this isolated and forested mountain country live the still little-known, warlike Motilón Indians. They have always put up fierce resistance to the encroachments of civilization. Their heavy, black, palm arrows have, in the past, been responsible for the death of many an oil man. Subsistence farming, stockraising, and hunting are their chief activities.

THE *LLANOS*

Between the Andes and the Orinoco river lies an immense (200 miles wide and 600 miles long), low (maximum elevation 700 ft.), nearly treeless plain called the *llanos*. This is a zone of great seasonal variation. From April to October heavy rains make the banks of the shallow streams overflow, flood the land, and drive the livestock to seek refuge in higher places to the north. Between November and March, on the other hand, the luxuriant, tall grasses are gradually seared and blackened, the rivers dry up, and the livestock are forced to migrate southward towards the Orinoco again in search of water and food.

The wet-dry extremes, the intense heat—Calabozo, for example, has an annual mean temperature of 88°F.—the

6

hordes of insect pests, and difficult communications in the rainy season, have kept the *llanos* a sparsely settled region. Only about 10 per cent. of the population lives here although it comprises over a third of the national territory. The exotic fauna of the region have been movingly described by Guillermo Zuloaga as follows:

The llanos are the Venezuelan region which stirs the imagination of sportsmen and hunters. Rivers and lagoons are filled with exotic fish; electric eels, which with their discharge can paralyze a bull or a horse; *caribes*, a small but ferocious and voracious fish, with jaws that possess the force of pincers, which travels in large schools and can eat an animal in a few seconds, leaving only the skeleton and boiling, blood-tinted water to mark the act; *payaras*, a fish gifted with terrible fangs; and catfish, of all forms and colors, some of which reach five feet in length and weigh hundreds of pounds.

Curious animals like the ant-eater, the *chiguire*, a giant rodent, and wild boars, are characteristic of the llanos.

The landscape, beautified by palm trees, is alive with birds. Among the most colorful are the very inquisitive *chenchena*, with reptilian characteristics; the *corocoro*, or scarlet ibis, with the color of fire; the herons, from the small egret formerly coveted for its plumage and today happily protected by game laws, to the great soldier heron; ducks of all kinds, from the native Royal duck to the small migratory ones which fly yearly into the llanos from the Arctic.[2]

For centuries, the economy of the *llanos* has centred in the cattle industry. After a season or two of plains grazing, most of the somewhat scrubby cattle are then driven over the interior range to the richer pastures in the vicinity of Maracay to be fattened for the market. Others are slaughtered in the *llanos* and the fresh meat is then flown into Caracas.

During the 1930's the economy of the eastern *llanos* began to undergo a fundamental transformation. This resulted from a rapid series of oil discoveries in the vast, deep sedimentary deposits that cover the entire region. The states

[2] *A Geographical Glimpse of Venezuela* (1957), p. 21.

of Anzoátegui and Monagas were soon dotted with oilfields, and petroleum became their chief export, as a third of the nation's oil—and most of its better-grade light oil—was produced here.

More recently, the agricultural possibilities of the central *llanos* have been improved. In 1956 the Government completed the construction of a dam across the Guarico river near Calabozo. The water now dammed up in the wet season to prevent flooding is used in the dry season to irrigate near-by rice and maize fields.

All the rivers of the *llanos* ultimately drain into the Orinoco. This huge river is some 1,600 miles long and is navigable by shallow-draught vessels all the way from the Atlantic Ocean to the Colombian border. Far upstream in the Guayana highlands about a third of its water is diverted to the Amazon via the Brazo Casiquiare. Nevertheless the Orinoco often reaches widths of more than half a mile, and in the rainy season the tides sometimes exceed forty feet at the mouth of the river.

THE GUAYANA HIGHLANDS

The fourth major geographical zone is the largest (45 per cent. of the nation's territory) but the least important. Less than 2 per cent. of Venezuela's people make their living in this vast region between the Orinoco river and the Brazilian border. The Guayana highlands are older and lower than the Andes, with maximum elevations of about 9,000 feet. Various igneous rock formations interspersed with semi-deciduous forests make up the landscape. The sparse population consists mainly of clusters of little-known Indians, some of them peaceful, others very savage.

Although this is a difficult area in which to make a living, it is rich in scenic grandeur. Concerning the Gran Sabana region in the extreme south-east, Zuloaga wrote:

Spectacular mountain masses rise up with their flat tops and vertical sides, their silhouettes reminding the viewer of the ruins of medieval castles. These are the '*tepuis*' of the Indians, the 'lost

8

world' of H. G. Wells. The Roraima, the Auyantepuí, the Yacapana, the Duida, with their smooth and vertical sides, are impossible to scale without the use of ladders. A region of rare beauty, the Gran Sabana is an unforgettable sight. From these high masses, whose tops pierce the clouds, descend the highest waterfalls in the world: Angel Falls, with an unobstructed drop of more than 3,000 feet, is the best known, but there are many others of equal beauty and breathtaking appearance.[3]

The metal-bearing formations of this rocky region, however, have been the chief lure for white man. In the late nineteenth century rich gold veins were discovered in the north-east. El Callao mine was for a time the chief gold producer in the world. There was also some placer mining, but by the turn of the century the gold boom had come to an end. In 1926 the perennial prospectors in the region discovered diamonds. These are of good quality but have never been very numerous or large.

The big mineral development here at present is the iron-ore industry. At El Pao and Cerro Bolívar in the north-eastern part of the region, on either side of the Caroní river, huge surface deposits of almost pure iron have been discovered. After the Second World War big American corporations (Bethlehem Steel and United States Steel) began intensive exploitation here.

FLORA AND FAUNA

Venezuela's great diversity in rainfall, elevation, and temperature produces a wide variety of plant and animal life. In the humid tropical zones are found cacao, bananas, coconuts, mangoes, palm and rubber trees, while the characteristic cacti and prickly pears grow in the dry areas. The semi-tropical regions (1,500–3,000 ft.) produce oranges, lemons, avocados, peaches, apricots, tobacco, sugar cane, cotton, and rice, and coffee, maize, beans, and potatoes are the chief crops of the temperate zone (above 3,000 ft.). The animals, except in the high mountains where there

[3] Zuloaga, pp. 27–29.

9

are bear and deer, are mostly those characteristic of tropical areas, such as jaguars, monkeys, ant-eaters, tapirs, crocodiles, alligators, boa constrictors, and anacondas. Numerous varieties of tropical to temperate birds, fish, and insects abound.

THE PEOPLE

At the time of the census of 26 November 1950, the population was 5,034,838. By 26 February 1961 it was 7,523,599.[4] If the current growth continues, the nation will have more than 10 million people by 1970.

Venezuela today is thus in the midst of a population explosion which has been set off by improving living standards, increasing birth-rates, declining mortality rates, and a strong post-Second World War wave of immigration. Between 1940 and 1955 the annual death-rate dropped by 44 per cent. (from $17 \cdot 2$ to $9 \cdot 7$ per 1,000) while the birth-rate increased by more than 20 per cent. (from $37 \cdot 2$ to $44 \cdot 8$ per 1,000).[5] During 1957 277,818 births and only 59,011 deaths were registered.[6] As the accompanying table illustrates, during the first century of nationhood, the population increased at a very slow rhythm, but since 1930 the tempo has accelerated every year.

Population of Venezuela 1830–1960
(millions)

1830	·7	1900	2·4
1840	1·1	1910	2·6
1850	1·3	1920	2·8
1860	1·6	1930	3·1
1870	1·7	1940	3·8
1880	1·9	1950	5·0
1890	2·1	1960	7·3

Source: Pocket Atlas of Venezuela, p. 12.

[4] Venezuela, Min. de Fomento, *IX Censo de población* (1962), p. 9.
[5] Venezuela, Min. de Relaciones Exteriores, *Venezuela en 1956* (1957), pp. 33–34.
[6] Venezuela, Dirección Gen. de Estadística, *Boletin mensual de estadística* (Dec. 1957), pp. 7–11.

The present population is expanding at an estimated 3·66 per cent. a year, which makes Venezuela one of the fastest-growing countries in the world. The nation has an extraordinarily young population. The 1961 census revealed that 60 per cent. of the people were under 25 and 80 per cent. under 40.

Nine-tenths of the population lives in the northern one-fifth of the republic, i.e. in the area comprising the Andes and the adjacent coastal lowlands. Venezuela is also one of the most heavily urbanized countries in Latin America with two out of three of its citizens living in communities of 1,000 or more. The largest cities are Caracas (1,234,130), Maracaibo (421,166), Barquisimeto (199,691), Valencia (163,601), Maracay (135,353), and San Cristóbal (98,777).[7]

The urbanization trend is relatively recent, for as late as 1936 nearly two-thirds of the population was still rural. Although part of the rapid urban growth is explained by the post-war influx of immigrants, by far the larger part is accounted for by a large-scale rural exodus stimulated by the better opportunities for work and living conditions offered in the cities. For instance, while the total population rose by 31 per cent. between 1941 and 1950, that of Caracas rose by 93 per cent.[8]

This internal migration has not followed strictly a farm to city pattern. More generally it can be described as a shift from centres of low economic activity to the more prosperous areas. Petroleum, mining, and commerce have drawn many people from the Andean states and Nueva Esparta into Zulia, Anzoátegui, Monagas, and the Federal District since 1936. In that year, for example, only 11 per cent. of the citizens of Venezuela were living outside their native states, but by 1950 22 per cent. were.[9]

---

[7] *IX Censo*, p. 8.
[8] Venezuela, Min. de Fomento, *Octavo censo general de población* (1957), vol. 12A, pp. 39–40.
[9] A. Uslar Pietri, *Sumario de economía venezolana*, 2nd ed. (1958), pp. 63–75.

RACE

Although the roots of Venezuela's language, religion, and culture are Spanish, the blood of its people is of varied origin. Over two-thirds of the population is mixed-blood, or mestizo, the product of the fusion of three races: the aboriginal, the white, and the black. About 20 per cent. are white, 9 per cent. are Negro, and less than 1 per cent. are Indian. The mestizos are dispersed throughout the republic, but the pure races tend to regional concentration—the whites in the larger cities in the Andes, the Negroes in the coastal lowlands, and the Indians in the remote forests of the Guayana highlands and the Sierra de Perijá.

Available statistical information indicates that the Indians are disappearing. In 1800 they reportedly made up 13 per cent. of the total population, but this percentage dropped to 7 by 1926, according to an official estimate, and to less than 1 by 1961. The Negroes are just about holding their own. They make up roughly the same percentage of the total population today as in 1800. After the slave trade ended in the early nineteenth century, no more Negroes came in until the 1920's, when large numbers came from the West Indies to find jobs in the growing oil industry. Since late in 1929, however, Negro immigrants have been barred from Venezuela by law. The only one of the three so-called pure races that may be tending to become a somewhat larger percentage of the total population is the white race. This is mainly due to the influx of the foreign oil men after 1920 and to European immigration after the Second World War.[10]

IMMIGRATION

For more than a century after independence Venezuela failed to develop a positive immigration policy. The nation was in a poor position to compete with countries such as the United States, Argentina, and Brazil in either the spon-

[10] See R. Fernández y Fernández, *Reforma agraria en Venezuela* (1948), pp. 162-9.

taneous, or the officially-financed, European immigration of the late nineteenth and early twentieth centuries. As a result, Venezuela's foreigners numbered only 45,000 (about 1 per cent. of the total population) as late as 1935, and most of these were Colombian farmers and traders, and United States, British, and Dutch oil men. In 1936 the Government, alarmed over the increasing inability of the nation to feed itself, drew up plans for attracting European farm immigrants, but none of the several schemes launched before the Second World War proved successful.

Not until after the war did large-scale immigration begin. A Government-sponsored immigration and land settlement programme, coupled with the existence of millions of displaced persons in Europe, brought in a stream of foreigners that increased from 1,780 for the year 1946 to 65,157 a decade later. By the end of 1957 foreigners in Venezuela numbered half a million and made up 8 per cent. of the total population. Of these, the largest group are Italians (31 per cent.), followed by Spaniards (28 per cent.), United States citizens (9 per cent.), Portuguese (7 per cent.), and Colombians (6 per cent.).[11] Venezuela attracted more European refugees after the Second World War than any country in Latin America except Argentina.

The Government's campaign to turn the immigrants into producers of food crops has been only moderately successful, for the majority preferred industrial and commercial pursuits in the cities. The 1950 census revealed that more than 40 per cent. of total foreign population was living in Caracas.[12] However, wherever they reside, the foreigners are contributing their skills and energies, and are thus playing a role in the economic, social, and cultural advance of Venezuela that is proportionately greater than their numbers.

[11] *Venezuela Up-to-date* (Venez. Embassy in Washington), Nov. 1957, pp. 9, 22.
[12] *8° censo*, vol. 12A, p. 116.

Venezuela

LIVING CONDITIONS

In some respects, Venezuela is one of the wealthiest nations in Latin America. Her vast petroleum and mineral treasures, ultra-modern cities, rich agricultural lands, motorways, and her prosperous, booming economy provide visual evidence of wealth. Her 1962 per capita income of $743—the highest in Latin America—affords statistical evidence of this.

And yet the very high cost of living and the extremely uneven distribution of wealth force over half the population to live at bare subsistence levels. According to the 1950 census figures, 1,706,321 (34 per cent. of the total population) were economically active. Of these, only 4 per cent. were employers. Of the remainder, 43 per cent. were wage-earners, 11 per cent. were salaried, 8 per cent. were engaged in non-remunerative service occupations, 27 per cent. were self-employed, and 7 per cent. were unclassified.[13]

Census figures do not reveal the income of the average worker, but an indication of his living conditions can be gleaned from housing statistics. Although three-quarters of Venezuela's dwellings were owner-occupied, more than one-half of these had thatched roofs and mud floors, less than one-third had running water, and the average size of home was under three rooms.[14]

Working and living conditions are best in the petroleum and iron industries, where wages are highest (about 25 bolivars per day in 1960) and housing, health, and education facilities are supplied by the foreign employer. However, the 40,000–50,000 workers thus employed are an *élite* group, forming less than 3 per cent. of the total labour force but taking home over half of the nation's money wages. Far less fortunate is the much more numerous and typical urban wage-earner employed in industry and commerce. Not only is his pay much lower, but all his needs

[13] Min. de Fomento, *8° censo de población: principales resultados nacionales* (1957), pp. 48–49.
[14] Ibid. p. 93.

14

have to come out of it. An indication of the inadequacy of
the urban wage-earner's pay is revealed by the fact that he
spends 48 per cent. of his entire income on food.[15] Even so,
his lot is not so miserable as that of the worker in the countryside, for despite difficult living conditions for the un-
skilled in Venezuela's growing cities, the rural exodus
shows few signs of abating.

Ownership of the choice agricultural holdings by a relatively small group of large owners has been characteristic
of rural Venezuela ever since the sixteenth century. The
1936 agricultural census, for instance, revealed that of the
635,600 farmers, 83 per cent. were renters, sharecroppers,
or day-labourers. And of the 17 per cent. who were proprietors, a small minority owned most of the best land. In
the three richest agricultural states of Aragua, Carabobo,
and Miranda the percentage of farmers classed as proprietors was only 3, 4, and 6 respectively. The pattern of
land concentration amongst the propertied was even more
revealing. In the state of Miranda, for example, 14 per cent.
of the proprietors owned 85 per cent. of the land.[16] The only
areas where latifundia are not a problem and family-size
holdings prevail are in the coffee-producing country of the
Andean slopes and in the newly formed agricultural settlements for immigrants in the northern *llanos*.

The problems of latifundia can perhaps best be illustrated from a table showing land distribution in the Venezuelan Andes and the coastal zone, where more than 95 per
cent. of all the nation's farms are to be found. Here
1,612,540 hectares of farm land was distributed amongst
43,000 proprietors as is shown on the table on p. 16.

Less than 1 per cent. of the proprietors owned more than
half of the farm acreage while 41 per cent. owned less than
3 per cent. These 1937 figures were still representative in
1960, but then began to change as agrarian reform
started.

[15] I.L.O., *Yearbook of Statistics, 1958*, p. 466.
[16] Fernández y Fernández, pp. 22–37.

Hectares	Per cent. of farms	Per cent. of acreage
Under 1	2·02	0·03
1–2	8·89	0·29
2–5	28·66	2·39
5–10	29·43	4·79
10–20	16·18	6·18
20–50	9·54	6·03
50–250	5·34	7·30
250–1,000	1·18	14·31
1,000–10,000	·52	30·45
10,000–25,000	·04	19·72
	100·00	100·00

Source: Venezuela, Min. de Agric. y Cría, *Censo agrícola y pecuario* (1941).

The typical Venezuelan agriculturist, making up 80 per cent. of the total farming population, is the *conuquero*.[17] He is a migratory peasant who raises subsistence crops such as corn, beans, and bananas on the mountain slopes which he periodically clears and burns. The *conuquero* is rarely a proprietor. Rather, for the use of the *conuco* he contributes to the owner either an annual rent, a share of the crop, or a portion of his labour. When the soil is exhausted, he moves elsewhere and constructs another crude shelter for his family.

CLASS

The pattern of landholding described above tells a good deal about the structure of rural society. Here a semimanorial system operates. There are essentially two classes —the wealthy minority group of large proprietors and the poverty-stricken, landless masses. The tax structure of the country reveals the traditional political dominance of the landlord element, for never in Venezuelan history have taxes been assessed on agricultural holdings.

In urban areas a more modern three-group type class structure has begun to develop. Particularly in the larger cities, between the wage-earning masses and the large merchants and property holders there are important middle-

[17] From *conuco*, a patch of ground formerly given to slaves.

income groups. These consist mainly of professional men, salaried corporation employees, government workers, and small business men. The middle class numbers about 15 per cent. of the economically active population.[18]

Social conditions in Venezuela in the 1950's have been summed up in an official United States government publication as follows:

Though recent years have brought great progress in improving the economic and social lot of the mass of the Venezuelan people, there is still a great gap between their situation and that of the landed aristocracy and the oil-wealthy. The rise of an industrial working class, the spread of popular education, and a growing middle class are all factors tending to obscure the lines between the classes of Venezuelan society.

Meanwhile a majority of the nation's population remains ill-fed, ill-clad, poorly housed, illiterate, and disease-weakened. Most rural families live in primitive huts without illumination, privacy, or decent sanitary facilities. With antiquated tools, they eke out a meager existence from the soil. Many city dwellers live in similar conditions, although slum clearance and improved sanitation are gradually restoring the most unsightly sections of Caracas and other major cities.

Politically and economically Venezuela is still dominated by a small segment of the society, an aristocracy whose standard of living is reflected in large urban estates, country clubs, modern office buildings, and luxurious apartment houses.[19]

Class is determined in Venezuela by race, family, and wealth. Although race prejudice is not strong, white is the predominant colour of the upper social strata, and the Negroes are at the bottom of the social scale. Inasmuch as over half of all births are illegitimate, the mere possession of a family name brings some prestige. Historic family names add immeasurably to social status, especially in the rural areas. In the cities, however, economic position, as reflected in housing, motor cars, bank balances, and real

[18] *8° censo: principales resultados*, pp. 48 f.
[19] U.S. Dept. of State, *Venezuela: Oil Transforms a Nation* (Washington, 1953), p. 5.

estate holdings, appears to be the principal determinant of class.

EDUCATION AND LITERACY

Though much progress has been made in recent years, Venezuela's educational facilities are still in need of expansion and improvement. In 1936 the illiteracy rate was 71 per cent., and only one-fifth of the school-age population was attending classes. According to the 1950 census, 62 per cent. of the population could neither read nor write, and half the children were without schools.[20] By 1963, illiteracy had been reduced to 25 per cent. and only 3 per cent. of the school-age children lacked educational facilities at the elementary levels of instruction.

Under Venezuelan law primary-school attendance is compulsory, and more than nine-tenths of the pupils (647,000) were found in 7,100 primary schools in 1957. That same year 266 secondary schools (44,000 pupils), 52 normal schools (6,280 pupils), and 3 national universities (Caracas, Zulia, and Mérida) provided the advanced educational facilities.[21] For higher education it is still customary for most Venezuelan parents who can afford it to send their children to the United States or Western Europe. Venezuela's elementary schools have been rapidly adopting more modern educational techniques since the war, but much of the old classical formalism and routine still prevailed in the *liceos* (secondary schools).

Until the Second World War Venezuelan universities adhered to the traditional emphasis upon training men in the liberal professions, and this training was restricted to people of means. In the post-war period, however, drastic reforms have come. Today the Government sets aside sufficient revenues not only to provide free higher education for all who care to attend, but also to pay professors enough to enable them to devote full time to scholarly pursuits. These advanced practices are in marked contrast to

[20] *8° censo*, vol. 12A, pp. 78, 95.   [21] *Pocket Atlas*, p. 12.

conditions in other Latin American countries. The Central University curriculum has also been broadened to include (in addition to the traditional faculties of medicine, law, philosophy, and letters) faculties of physical and mathematical science, dentistry, pharmacy, chemistry, economics and social science, agronomy, veterinary medicine, and journalism.

HEALTH

Venezuela's health facilities leave much to be desired. The majority of the population still lacks adequate medical care and social-welfare services. Yet bad as present conditions are, they were much worse in the past. Until 1911, when the first national health office was opened, the Government assumed no responsibility for the bodily well-being of the citizenry. A second minor step was taken in 1936 when a Ministry of Social Welfare was created, but it was not until after the Second World War that Venezuela's Government began to develop national programmes of hospital construction and disease control. By 1957 the Government directed 46 health centres engaged in preventive work and 59 hospitals, and was actively promoting campaigns to combat tropical and venereal diseases. Malaria has been virtually eliminated. Notable progress has also been made in the fight against tuberculosis, for many years the second deadliest disease. By 1959 the number of deaths from T.B. was less than half the 1945 rate, and it had been reduced to fifth place among fatal diseases. Dysentery has long ranked first of these, and despite the Government's sanitation programmes, more Venezuelans continue to die of it than any other malady.

Nutrition is, of course, related to the problem of disease. A virtually complete absence of such staples as meat, milk, and butter, and insufficient calories were notorious amongst the poorer people down to the end of the Second World War. Since then, however, a vigorous attack on the problem of hunger has been made, and by 1957 Venezuela was producing enough foodstuffs to provide 2,530 calories per person per day and importing 15–20 per cent. more. Even though the food supply is not evenly distributed and the diet is top-heavy with starches, the Venezuelan people are certainly not starving.

In government hospitals, medical and surgical services are free to the poor. Social insurance helps to pay the costs of many wage-earners and salaried people. The Government's food-growing and health-improvement programmes have been largely responsible for the rapid post-war drop in the death-rate. For a Venezuelan born in 1943, life expectancy was 46 years; in 1955 it was 51.[22]

RELIGION

Venezuela is Catholic, and an overwhelming majority of its citizens profess that faith. Catholicism is the official religion of the country, and the Government exercises the right of patronage over high Church officials. It also subsidizes the lower clergy and helps to pay church maintenance costs. Administratively, the republic is divided into two archdioceses, one at Caracas, the other at Mérida. The secular clergy are trained in Caracas, the regulars abroad.

Although Church and state have not been separated, ecclesiastical influence in the Government is slight. For instance, in the public schools, Catholic instruction may be given only at the express request of the parent. In politics, the influence of the Catholic Church, though decisively broken in the late nineteenth century by the anti-clerical decrees of Dictator Antonio Guzmán Blanco, is growing.

Taking advantage of the freedom of worship guaranteed in the Constitution, several Protestant sects have established churches. Except among the primitive Indians, however, the expansion of their influence has been slow.

[22] Min. de Rel. Ext., *Venezuela en 1956*, p. 112.

Chapter II

HISTORY TO 1945

CHRISTOPHER COLUMBUS discovered Venezuela on his third voyage to America. He spent the first two weeks of August 1498 exploring the delta region of the Orinoco river and the shores of the Paria peninsula. A year later, a follow-up expedition commanded by Alonso de Ojeda covered the same route, and then proceeded along Venezuela's northern coast to Lake Maracaibo. Here the Indian village huts built on stilts in the shallow water reminded the Spanish explorers of a miniature Venice; hence they christened the land Little Venice, or Venezuela.

The first of Spain's New World mainland colonies to be discovered and explored, Venezuela was one of the last to be conquered and developed. The low regard of the mother country for this colony stemmed both from environmental impediments to effective colonization and from the lure of other regions wealthier in human and material resources, such as Mexico and Peru.

Venezuela's Indians were primitive. Though probably descended from a common ancestor, their civilization was far below that of the Incas of Peru or the Chibchas of neighbouring Colombia. The most advanced Indians in Venezuela were the farming tribes of the Andes and the northeast coast region; the most backward were the nomadic hunting and fishing tribes that roamed the Lake Maracaibo basin and the *llanos*. In the central coastal area lived both nomadic and agricultural groups. Many of the tribes were cannibalistic; nearly all of them were warlike.

The initial half-century of European contact with Venezuela resulted in no effective colonization, primarily because the early interests of the white man were confined to the exploitation of pearls, gold, and slaves. During the first thirty years after the discovery, Spanish activities were limited to slave hunting on the north-east coast and pearl fishing off the adjacent islands. A few small settlements were founded, but these were abandoned as soon as profits dwindled.

In 1528 the centre of activity shifted to western Venezuela. In that year Charles V mortgaged the whole colony to the German banking house of Welser, whose interest was primarily gold. It spent the next generation in a futile search for rich cities and mines, whereupon the enterprise collapsed, and Venezuela returned to Spanish control once more.

It was then obvious that Venezuela's success as a colonial enterprise would have to depend upon the occupation and use of the land. The conquest, undertaken in the latter half of the sixteenth century, was slow and difficult. Since the scattered Indian groups had no political unity, separate wars had to be waged against almost every tribe. Moreover, low-priority Venezuela was unable to obtain royal troops. Geographical obstacles added to the problems. Nevertheless, the Spaniards were equal to the challenge. Step by step they subjugated the red man and put him to work on their farms, and they founded cities. By the end of the century, in contrast to the several small settlements that existed in 1545, twenty cities dotted the Andes and the Caribbean coast, and these regions were now effectively occupied by Spanish farmers. Caracas, founded in 1567, was the most prosperous city and province.

The conquest was far from complete by the end of the sixteenth century. The *llanos* and the Maracaibo basin, inhabited primarily by nomadic Indians, still had to be reduced. In this arduous task the coercion of the conquistadores gave way to the peaceful persuasion of the Catholic missionaries. The latter's attempts to Christianize and protect the Indians on the north-east coast in the early sixteenth century had been frustrated by the avarice of the

Spanish slave hunters. In the mid-seventeenth century, however, when the demands for opening up new areas for settlement could not be satisfied by the civil authorities, the friars were called back. Capuchins, Jesuits, Franciscans, and Dominicans made heroic efforts to transfer into the wild interior the religion, language, culture, and laws of Spain, and though they indeed made progress, much remained to be done at the end of the colonial period.

Even before the missionaries took charge of the Spanish occupation in the interior, the secular arm of the Catholic Church had built up a great power and prestige in the settled mountain and coastal areas. Not only did it dominate in matters ecclesiastical, but it also monopolized education. And, as the Church began to accumulate lands, it exerted considerable economic power as well. In addition, its political influence was enhanced by the frequent royal practice of appointing the clergy to high governmental office. However, ecclesiastical power was a localized phenomenon. The Church displayed no administrative unity in the colony as a whole, and the fierce rivalries and jurisdictional disputes amongst the hierarchy undermined the broad institutional strength that might have come through union.

Factionalism and decentralization also characterized the colonial government and administration of Venezuela. The colony, ever a marginal political entity in Spain's New World Empire, was generally under the rule of more important neighbouring areas. During the sixteenth and seventeenth centuries Venezuela was under the jurisdiction of the Audiencia of Santo Domingo. In the eighteenth century it was placed under the Viceroyalty of New Granada at Bogotá. However, neither the audiencia nor the viceroy exercised any measure of effective control over the remote Government in Caracas.

Furthermore, the governor of Caracas was unable to exercise much influence over the six other provinces. In addition, the municipalities, from the time of their founding, were ruled by their own *cabildos* (municipal councils), which bodies successfully resisted, until the end of the colonial period, the attempts of the provincial officials to render them heteronomous. Only for a brief period following the establishment of the Captaincy-General of Venezuela in 1777, independent of the viceroy and directly under the Crown, did colonial Venezuela experience a measure of administrative unity.[1] The authority of the Captain-General at Caracas, however, lasted too short a time to weaken appreciably the long tradition of provincial and municipal autonomy.

The development of the colonial economy went through various phases.[2] Since little-valued Venezuela was at first not even a stopping place for the annual Spanish merchant fleets, a diversified, self-sufficient economy grew up with the conquest. From the beginning the colonists produced their own staples such as maize, beans, wheat, and beef. By the end of the sixteenth century Venezuela began to yield such highly valued tropical crops as tobacco, sugar, cocoa, and indigo, and by the early seventeenth century the herds of cattle had multiplied to the point where it was possible to produce for export large quantities of hides.

The potential for lucrative trade with Venezuela was appreciated earlier by other European nations than by Spain. Though the prevailing mercantilist system proclaimed trade with outsiders illegal, Spain's foreign competitors would not be denied. By the end of the sixteenth century French and English privateers and smugglers were making regular trips to Venezuelan ports. At the turn of the century Dutch merchant fleets began exploiting the salt pans on the north-east coast and early in the seventeenth century began supplying Negro slaves in exchange for cacao and tobacco.

The success of Spain's rivals encouraged the mother

[1] Venezuela had first been established as a separate captaincy-general in 1731. In the period 1740–77 however, she was a part of the Viceroyalty of New Granada.

[2] The best work on this subject is Eduardo Arcila Farías, *Economía colonial de Venezuela* (1946).

country to open up direct trade between Seville and Venezuela in the early seventeenth century, but European wars and poorly defended Caribbean coasts assured others of the lion's share of Venezuela's exports. Heavy European demands for cacao and tobacco inclined the farmers more and more towards monoculture, the result being that Venezuela had to begin importing staples by the end of the seventeenth century. Trade disruption caused by the War of the Spanish Succession (1702–13) resulted in acute food shortages.

During the eighteenth century the Crown made determined efforts to bring Venezuela into the Spanish commercial orbit. For this purpose a monopoly trading company, the Real Compañía Guipuzcoana (better known as the Caracas Company), was chartered in 1728. Its Basque merchant directors were granted not only economic control but also political power over Venezuela. For a full half century the Caracas Company displayed remarkable success in curbing foreign competition, developing cacao, cotton, and hide production for export, and encouraging domestic manufacturing.

Unhappily, the success of the Caracas Company depended upon oppression of the Venezuelan people. The company merchants paid the agricultural producers as little as possible, yet fixed the prices of the wares they sold in Venezuela so as to extort the maximum profit. Widespread dissatisfaction and resistance forced relaxation of the monopoly in 1781, and a few years later the Caracas Company disappeared. Till the end of the colonial period, the Venezuelan producers again thrived, but so did the non-Spanish traders. Royal intendants, sent over in the late eighteenth century to look after the interests of the Spanish treasury, were unable to prevent illegal trade in the face of international wars and the colonists' determination to profit from their new-found commercial freedom.

Colonial society was a caste system. Status was based upon colour, position, and wealth. At the top of the social pyramid was the white race, which never amounted to more than about 15 per cent. of the total population. A small group of royal bureaucrats and Spanish clergymen enjoyed the greatest prestige, but the creoles, the descendants of the conquistadores, owned the land and dominated local politics.

Miscegenation was so common from the earliest days of the colony that by the end of the colonial period over half the population were *pardos*, or mixed bloods. Like all groups except the whites, the *pardos* were without wealth, political influence, or social prestige. They congregated in the cities or lived in the *llanos*.

The isolated interior was the home of the Indians, whose numbers were appreciably reduced by miscegenation and by labour exploitation. At the end of the eighteenth century Indians constituted less than 10 per cent. of the total population.

The Negro, unlike the Indian, increased rather than diminished in numbers. First introduced in the early seventeenth century, they made up a fifth of the total population by the end of the eighteenth. The great majority of the Negroes were slaves on the coastal plantations.

THE INDEPENDENCE MOVEMENT, 1810–30

Venezuela's fight for freedom from Spain in the early nineteenth century was something more than a mere regional episode in the larger Latin American movement for independence. Venezuela was rather the spearhead of the whole movement in South America. Her people launched the first successful rebellion against Spain. Her revolutionary leaders and soldiers freed not only Venezuela but also played leading roles in the liberation of Colombia, Ecuador, Peru, and Bolivia.

Many forces were at work in the late eighteenth century impelling Venezuela towards a break with the mother country. Influences from outside such as the new liberal, intellectual currents of the European Enlightenment and the example of successful revolutions by the thirteen English colonies and by the people of France had their effects, but the deeper causes for separatism were internal. The spirit of liberty had long thrived in the *cabildos*, and the creoles who dominated these local governing bodies bitterly resisted Spain's late eighteenth-century efforts to tighten her political hold over the colony. Also, after two centuries of royal neglect, Venezuelans resented the Crown's efforts to extort ever larger profits from the colony. The peninsular officials were the agents of political oppression and economic exploitation, and the consequent antagonism between them and the creoles probably contributed more than anything else to the ultimate break with Spain.

The first serious creole resistance occurred in 1749 when a group of landholders demonstrated against the excesses of the Caracas Company. In 1797 a major conspiratorial movement, which had independence as its aim, was nipped in the bud by the Spanish authorities.

During the first decade of the nineteenth century revolutionary activities were dominated by Francisco de Miranda, the principal precursor of the Latin American independence movement. This dogged creole, the son of a Caracas merchant, was a man with a mission. Appreciating the mother country's superior strength, his efforts were concentrated upon obtaining foreign assistance, and whenever Spain was at odds with England, France, or the United States, Miranda would appeal for their support. In desperation, in 1806 he attempted, with wholly inadequate resources, an invasion of the Venezuelan coast. Frustrated by effective Spanish defences, he returned to England to prepare for a new attempt.

The immediate cause of the independence movement was the collapse of royal authority in Venezuela following Napoleon Bonaparte's conquest of the Iberian Peninsula in 1808–10. Two groups—Napoleon and the Central Spanish Junta, which had been formed to resist him—vied for the

27

colonial power of the deposed King Charles IV, but the Venezuelan creoles rejected the overtures of both. Instead they seized the opportunity to assume control themselves. In April 1810 the creoles of Caracas deposed the Spanish governor. Joined by creole leaders from six other provinces, they set up a governing junta, and also, somewhat later, a national Congress. On 5 July 1811 the junta declared Venezuela independent and began drawing up a constitution for the new nation.

That this precipitate action by the native white aristocracy did not have the support of other social groups soon became apparent. The traditional political apathy of the submerged Negro and Indian elements remained undisturbed by the events of 1810–11. To the majority *pardo* element, however, the transference of political power to the already socially and economically dominant creole class was viewed with considerable misgiving, for the peninsular officials had customarily moderated the severe conflicts and antagonisms between the native whites and the mixed-bloods. Consequently the *pardos*, except in the Caracas area, fought on the side of the royalists until late in the war.

And yet, despite the initial popular indifference or hostility to their cause, the creoles might have won much more easily had they been less inept. Long accustomed as they were to local autonomy, they were psychologically incapable of achieving the unity and co-ordinated effort necessary to the success of a separatist movement. Beginning with their rather foolish promulgation of a federalist Constitution in 1811, the creole leaders marched rapidly down the path of error. Suspicious of the ambitions of Miranda, they failed to grant him, until too late, the powers he needed to prosecute the war vigorously against the growing royalist forces. In addition, because of the disruption of trade and poor fiscal management, an economic crisis was soon upon the country. Less than ten months after the declaration of independence the first republic fell. On 26 March 1812 the *coup de grace* was delivered in the form of an earthquake which razed the patriot cities but did little harm to the royalist strongholds. Soon afterwards the patriot resistance came to an end.

Though the royalist clergy seized upon the earthquake as proof of divine disapproval of rebellion against the Spanish king, the Church was by no means united against the patriots. Not that it made much difference, for by the beginning of the nineteenth century its prestige and influence had fallen so low that it was no longer a decisive factor. The sectionalism characteristic of Church policy merely reflected, of course, the regional political strength of the royalists and patriots.[3]

The backbone of patriot strength was the great spine of the Andes, where the creole landholders lived, and the Caracas area, where even the masses rallied to the independence movement. The royalists, however, held firm in the north-east and in the *llanos* where they exploited the *pardo* hatred of the wealthy whites. The Spanish were also able gradually to set the Negro slaves and even some of the Indians against their creole masters. Thus the royalists staved off the threatened political schism between Venezuela and the mother country—for a decade at least—by perverting the separatist movement into a social upheaval.

With the collapse of the first republic the leadership of the patriot remnants passed to Simón Bolívar, a young man destined to become the father of Venezuela. He was not only a military genius, but also a persuasive orator, a shrewd politician, a great statesman, and a staunch republican idealist. His talents and achievements overshadowed those of all his compatriots in the Latin American independence movement. His energy and determination were unmatched.

Bolívar was born in Caracas, of wealthy creole parents, in 1783. Though orphaned at the age of nine, he was educated by capable tutors. After serving briefly in the Spanish

[3] The best work in English on the role of the Church is Mary Watters, *A History of the Church in Venezuela, 1810–1930* (1933).

Venezuela

army in Venezuela, he went to Spain when sixteen years old to complete his education. In Paris, early in 1802, he was impressed by the victorious Napoleon and by republican France. In the mother country he fell in love, and at the age of nineteen returned with his bride to settle down on one of his estates. His wife's sudden death, however, changed everything. To allay his misery, Bolívar spent the years 1804–7 travelling and studying in Europe, and it was here that he became imbued with a mission to liberate his people from Spain. Though not a member of the 1810 junta, he was a prime mover behind the 1811 declaration of independence, and second in command to Miranda under the first republic.

After the collapse of the first republic, Bolívar fled to Colombia. There his brilliant military services on behalf of the patriots, and his convincing arguments that the independence of Venezuela was essential to Colombian nationhood, won him the command of an expedition to invade Venezuela from the west. By mid-1813 he had crossed the border. His campaign was abetted by Spanish oppression and the consequent outbreaks of new revolutionary uprisings, particularly in eastern Venezuela. Convinced that victory would hinge upon converting social warfare into a political struggle, he issued his famous 'war to the death' decree to all Spaniards and their partisans. By August 1813 General Bolívar's victorious army had reached Caracas, where he was proclaimed Liberator of his country.

But complete liberation was still a long way off, for the Spaniards were still strong on the coast, and the *pardo* population of the *llanos* had still to be converted. The royalists, still exploiting the social issue, won over the *llaneros* with promises of war booty and racial equality. The result was that in less than a year Bolívar and the patriots were again driven from the capital. Thus the second republic fell in 1814 as suddenly as the first, and for much the same reasons.

Once more Bolívar fled to Colombia, but this time a large Spanish army, fresh from the Peninsular Wars against Na-

poleon in Europe, made this area unsafe, whereupon he fled
first to Jamaica, then to Haiti. In exile, he now realized that
support of the majority *pardo* element was a *sine qua non* for
success of the independence movement, and that, because
Spain's hands were no longer tied in Europe, the patriots
would need foreign assistance.

The new strategy was to invade from the east. Bolívar's
landing in north-eastern Venezuela in December 1816
brought the patriot underground to the surface. Soon afterwards *llanero* chieftain José Antonio Páez joined the patriot
cause, and headquarters were set up near the mouth of the
Orinoco. Here the much sought-after European aid, principally English volunteer veterans of the Napoleonic Wars,
began to flow in. The year 1817 was a turning-point. Thereafter the Spanish defenders could never cope with the steady
growth of nationalism amongst the Venezuelan masses and
the inflow of European manpower, military advisers, and
equipment.

By mid-1819 the Liberator was ready to resume the offen-
sive. By August his army had scaled the Andes and freed
Colombia. The way was now clear for the final conquest
of Venezuela. In June 1821 Spanish resistance was decisively broken at the Battle of Carabobo, just west of Caracas.

Venezuela was finally free, but she had paid dearly for
that freedom. She had suffered more than any other Latin
American country. Eleven years of warfare had cost her the
lives of one-fourth of her entire population. Her social structure had been upset by the Spanish-induced class warfare.
Her economy had been ruined in the fighting.

It was to be another nine years before a truly independent
national status was achieved. In the spring of 1821 delegates
from Venezuela and Colombia had met at the border town
of Cúcuta to arrange for joining their territories into a single
nation such as had been envisaged by Bolívar several years
previously. Immediately following the news of victory at
Carabobo, the Cúcuta Congress, embodying in modified
form Bolívar's ideas, proclaimed the formal union of Col-

ombia and Venezuela and thus formed the new Republic of Gran Colombia. A Constitution was framed, the capital was fixed at Bogotá, and provision was made to add Ecuador to the republic once that area was freed. Bolívar was elected President and Francisco de Paula Santander, a Colombian, Vice-President.

However, as soon as the restless Liberator dashed off to devote his talents to freeing Ecuador, Peru, and Bolivia, deep-seated separatist tendencies in Venezuela became apparent. The municipalities of Caracas and Valencia began expressing reservations over a constitution which placed Venezuela in a subordinate position to the central Government in Bogotá, and General Páez, military commander of the Venezuelan area, began showing a marked disinclination to take orders from Santander. When the latter issued a call for troops, Venezuelans showed little disposition to volunteer their services outside their own region. By 1826 the Venezuelan military and the creole landed aristocracy, united behind Páez, had assumed a position of autonomy. They made it unmistakably clear that they would no longer comply with orders emanating from Bogotá.

Alarmed by news of the threatened dissolution of Gran Colombia, Bolívar, whose armies were just completing the task of liberating Peru and Bolivia, returned from Lima to Bogotá and thence to Caracas. Faced with the autonomous demands of the Venezuelan leaders, it was obvious to him that drastic constitutional reforms were the only hope of salvaging Gran Colombia. He promptly called a constituent convention, which met at Ocaña, Colombia, in April 1828. Here Bolívar's centralist principles were undermined not only by Santander and the federalist delegates from Colombia, but also by most of the delegates from his native country. The discussions proved fruitless, and the convention broke up.

To save Gran Colombia from dissolution, Bolívar's partisans urged him to assume dictatorial powers, which he did in August 1828, but it was too late. General Páez's supreme power in Venezuela could not be successfully challenged, and the Liberator's task of building a viable Government was rendered insuperable by pervasive federalist tendencies in both Colombia and Ecuador. The new constitutional convention convoked in January 1830 in Bogotá proved but a gathering to pronounce the failure of the Gran Colombia ideal. Centralist sentiment was in the minority. Venezuelan delegates did not even bother to attend. Instead, Páez convoked a special constitutional convention to meet in Valencia. Thus the determination of Venezuela to separate had been made irrevocable. Soon afterwards Ecuador withdrew, and Gran Colombia collapsed. The disappointed and disillusioned Liberator resigned and prepared to go into exile, but he became ill and died on the Colombian coast in 1830.

Regional realities had thus triumphed over Bolívar's grand national idealism. The long tradition of colonial autonomy, the military feudalism that grew up out of the brutal wars for independence, the determination of the propertied *élite* to exercise local control, the personal ambitions of General Páez—all these factors inexorably worked towards independent nationhood for Venezuela.

THE CONSERVATIVE OLIGARCHY, 1830–48

Though the problems Venezuela's first national Government had to deal with during its eighteen years of tenure were tremendous, its successes in meeting them were notable. Small wonder that Venezuelan historians often refer to the 1830–48 period as a sort of golden age in their national political life, for in contrast to the troublous times that preceded and followed it, this was an era of political stability, economic progress, and honest administration.

Leader of the Government of the so-called Conservative Oligarchy was the same *llanero* general who had controlled the nation's destinies ever since 1821. It was Páez who guaranteed the constitutional order established in 1830. It

was he who called to order the provincial *caudillos* whose
ambitions had been so inflated during the war for independence. On several occasions during the 1830's he personally
led his army against his erstwhile colleagues. Páez was the
nation's first President (1831–5), and he was re-elected for
another four-year term in 1839. In the years when he did
not actually occupy the presidential office he remained,
until 1848, the power behind the scenes. Only men amen-
able to him might administer, and only policies approved
by him could be implemented. Yet government in the Páez
era was not just a one-man régime, for the general had made
an alliance with the country's wealthy citizenry. He had
confidence in their abilities and allowed them to formulate
plans for running the country.

At the 1830 Constituent Assembly in Valencia were the
landowners—proprietors of the Andean coffee estates, of
the coastal cacao, tobacco, sugar, and cotton plantations,
and of the *llano* cattle ranches. With them sat the country's
wealthy merchants and leading professional men. The result of their labours was the Constitution of 1830, a document which reflected the social and political philosophy of
its creators. The state was to be a mixed centralist-federalist
entity, republican in form. There were to be moderate property qualifications for voting and substantial ones for holding political office. The manumission age for slaves was
raised from eighteen years to twenty-one. Legislation on
freedom of contracts permitted the ruling creditor class to
charge unlimited interest, and stern legal means were provided for collection of debts. To preserve their governing
monopoly, the propertied, moneyed, and educated minori-
ties imposed—and enforced—the death penalty for political
crimes.

Final assurance of the supremacy of the state was
achieved by stripping special privileges from both the
Church and the army. The former lost its tax immunities,
its tithing rights, its religious and educational monopolies,
and its unlimited powers of patronage. The army was shorn

of its autonomy and rendered subservient to the central Government.

Stability thus assured, remarkable progress was made towards reconstructing the war-torn economy. Wagon roads constructed in the interior facilitated internal commerce and promoted the export of agricultural commodities. German immigrants were brought in to farm unoccupied highland areas in the north-central part of the country. Honest and capable ministers put finances in order. They amortized a third of the national debt and firmly established the nation's credit abroad.

After a decade of rule by the Conservative Oligarchy, the first cracks began to appear in the monolithic political structure they had created. There were several contributing factors. The civilian element was becoming restless because the military clique had monopolized the office of President. Moreover, within the civilian oligarchy tensions began to develop between the dominant landholding faction and the commercial and professional minority. But probably the most important factor of all was the growing popular antagonism to the obvious attempts on the part of the Conservative Oligarchy to reconstruct the colonial system, with a Venezuelan general substituted for the Spanish king, with creole lawyers substituted for the Spanish ministers, and with the colonial society and economy preserved intact.

All these factors contributed to the rise of an opposition Liberal Party. It was founded in 1840 by disgruntled non-agrarian Conservatives. Their chief spokesman was Antonio Leocadio Guzmán. Minister of the Interior under the Conservative Oligarchy during the 1830's, his political intrigues finally brought dismissal, whereupon he founded the Liberal Party and the Liberal newspaper *El Venezolano*.

A campaign was launched to stir the populace to action against the 'selfish' and 'vicious' Government of the Conservative Oligarchy. Demands were made for emancipation of the slaves, extension of the franchise, limitation of interest rates, and abolition of capital punishment. Páez's autocratic rule was condemned, and the economic difficulties experienced during the early 1840's, though primarily caused by world conditions, were described as a consequence of the 'stupid' policies of the Conservatives.

In the face of the mounting agitation, the Conservative Oligarchy found it increasingly necessary to resort to force and electoral fraud in order to resist the Liberal challenge. The press was muzzled, and opposition politicians were persecuted. The political crisis began to become acute soon after the 1846 elections. These were won by General José Tadeo Monagas, whom the Conservatives had put up as the man most likely to defend their position and maintain stability. Monagas, however, soon revealed that he had no interest in preserving the privileged political position of the Conservative Oligarchy. In fact he seemed to have little interest in anything save his own power. First, he built up his military backing; then he brought the political issue to a head in March of 1848 by ousting the Conservative ministers and replacing them with Liberals. When Congress tried to impeach him, he had a mob intimidate that body. When Páez was provoked to rebel, Monagas was ready for him, defeated him in 1848, and exiled him in 1850.

LIBERALISM AND FEDERALISM, 1848–72

Monagas's desertion of, and defeat of, the Conservatives in 1848 inaugurated a decade of rule by the so-called Liberal Oligarchy. Actually the period 1848–58 was one of dictatorial rule by General José Tadeo Monagas, who took limited advice from the leading Liberals. Thus such party planks as the abolition of slavery, extension of the suffrage, the abolition of capital punishment for political crimes, and limitation of interest rates became law, but many such measures were made meaningless by the tyrannical personalism practised by the President.

For example, extension of the suffrage was made a hollow gesture by the *caudillo's* refusal to respect free electoral processes and parliamentary liberties. The manumission law of 1854 'freed' 40,000 slaves, but the newly emancipated were devoid of political rights and economic opportunity, and experienced virtually no change in their social position till Monagas fell from power.

Monagas's dictatorship, unlike that of Páez, was a predatory one. He seems to have had little concern for economic or social reforms likely to promote national welfare. Integrity disappeared in Government; the economy began to stagnate and decay; continuous deficit financing ruined the nation's credit.

Obsessed with the maintenance and enhancement of his personal power, Monagas met any sort of political activity with brutality. His tyranny was made to pervade the entire republic through his provincial military satraps. In 1850 José Tadeo sponsored the candidacy of his brother, José Gregorio, who dutifully guarded the presidency for four years, and then returned it to the *de facto* ruler in 1854. José Tadeo then, irritated by the provisions in the 1830 Constitution, framed a new one in 1857, which extended the presidential term to six years and placed no restrictions upon re-election.

This blatant attempt to establish a Monagas dynasty was too much for the Liberals. They joined the Conservative opposition and, with the help of defectors from the army, brought the dictatorship to an end in March 1858. This was the first successful rebellion in Venezuela's national history, but it set off a chain of revolutionary uprisings against Governments in power during the next five years. The turmoil arose because the Liberals and Conservatives, though capable of united action against a common enemy, were unable to agree upon a coalition Government. General Julian Castro was selected as compromise President in 1858, but his partiality towards the Conservatives soon began to split the coalition administration. The new 1858 Constitution, which ignored most Liberal demands, made the schism complete. Provincial *caudillos* associated with the Liberal Party, particularly General Juan Falcón in the west, then rose against the Caracas Government, and the five-year Federalist War ensued. The rebel cry was for 'federalism' as opposed to 'centralism', which the Conservatives demanded in the 1858 Constitution.

Initially, 'federalism' seems to have been an issue artificially created by the Liberal publicist, Antonio Guzmán Blanco (son of the Liberal Party founder), in an attempt to gain additional supporters. Already backing for the Liberal Party was substantial amongst the mass of the people, whose principal economic and social oppressors were counted in the ranks of the Conservative Party. Federalism also appealed to the always considerable regional and provincial sentiments in the country even amongst many Conservative partisans. All the same, as the war progressed the populace increasingly came to equate federalism with democracy and with economic and social reform. The result was that the Federalist War began to turn into a social upheaval.

The complicated course of that war is almost impossible to follow. It is sufficient to say that the conflict was exceedingly bloody and that the central Government changed hands various times. During the war the desperate Conservatives recalled General Páez, and this gallant old soldier for two years (1861–3) succeeded in maintaining his party in control at the centre. However, in 1863 final victory went to the Federalist forces led by Generals Juan Falcón and Antonio Guzmán Blanco.

Falcón then became the duly elected President, and the Federalist principles for which the Liberals had been fighting were incorporated into the 1864 Constitution. Both the President and the Constitution contributed to the national disintegration that followed in the 1864–70 period. Falcón had little interest in running the country; instead he carelessly delegated responsibility to irresponsible subordinates. The Federalist Constitution, instead of bringing the hoped-for local freedom, generally resulted in local tyrannies. Regional *caudillos*, in league with all the propertied elements that feared social upheaval, set up a kind of provincial political feudalism. Thus the hopes of the masses were effectively throttled by force of arms as predatory militarists became their masters.

Attempts by the central Government to bring some kind of order out of the political chaos, to halt the venality of the local *caudillos*, to get the various parts of the country to co-operate in fostering the national progress and welfare failed because of inept leadership and excessive federalism.

As the mismanagement of the Liberals became more notorious, the Conservatives planned their come-back. By force of arms they succeeded under the leadership of the former 'Liberal' tyrant José Tadeo Monagas, but his triumph merely opened the flood-gates of civil war once more. The ensuing chaos paved the way to power for Antonio Guzmán Blanco, the Liberal politician-general who was to pacify the country and run it dictatorially for the next generation.

ANTONIO GUZMÁN BLANCO

The Federalist War and its confusing aftermath provided the opportunity for the political rise of Guzmán Blanco. A child of the liberalism begun by his father, he gave expression to such principles during the fighting. He also demonstrated a talent for soldiering, and rapidly rose to the rank of general. In addition, he showed an aptitude for diplomacy, first in getting rival Liberal generals to co-operate, then in arranging peace with the Conservatives in 1863. The manifold abilities of this young man were further demonstrated when many of his ideas were incorporated in the 1864 Constitution. At the time of its promulgation he was in London, as fiscal agent of the Falcón Government, successfully negotiating a £1½ million loan. During 1865 his administrative talents were revealed when President Falcón permitted him to tighten the control of the central

Government, reorganize the nation's finances, and launch a programme of economic development. Suspicious of this brilliant young man's ambitions, Falcón sent Guzmán Blanco back to Europe on official business, but the Conservative revolution of 1868 offered him the opportunity to return and take charge.

Guzmán Blanco's triumphal entry into Caracas at the head of the Liberal forces in April 1870 brought an abrupt halt to the instability, civil war, political chaos, and economic stagnation which Venezuela had endured since 1858. A determined man with a definite programme was at the helm. Taking the field himself, Guzmán Blanco pacified the country by destroying all the Conservative revolutionary bands in less than two years. While thus engaged, he found time to launch a vigorous reform programme firmly based upon Liberal Party principles.

Two months after assuming power he ordered the establishment of a system of public primary education throughout the country. He arranged for new taxes to finance it and vowed not to rest till every city had an elementary school. In addition, state support was given to secondary and professional schools and to the Central University in Caracas. Guzmán Blanco put the anti-clerical principles of his party promptly into practice by making war on the Catholic Church, that traditional bastion of conservatism. He exiled the archbishop, closed the convents, confiscated Church properties, abolished ecclesiastical privileges, cut off state subsidies, proclaimed religious liberty, legalized civil marriage, and even threatened to establish a national church independent of the Pope.

Sweeping economic reforms gave further evidence of the new ruler's apparent devotion to Liberal Party principles. The nation's credit, ruined by twelve years of civil war and instability, was restored by a special bond issue and a complete fiscal reorganization. Customs duties were drastically reduced, resulting in increased revenue through a much higher volume of trade, and graft was sharply curbed as

Guzmán Blanco insisted on honesty and efficiency on the part of his subordinates.

Once the Government's financial house had been set in order, the new President launched a vigorous public works programme designed to develop the nation's economy. The major cities were modernized, port facilities were improved, and a network of interior communications was begun by the construction of main roads, railways, and telegraph lines. Further stimulus to material progress was given by encouraging foreign investment through the granting of liberal concessions for the exploitation of natural resources.

Finally, once the country was effectively pacified in 1872, provision was made for the attainment of political liberalism by a Constitution that provided for democratic, representative government, universal suffrage, and the direct election of the President. Guzmán Blanco was the overwhelming popular choice for President in the April 1873 elections, and he was backed by a Congress that unanimously supported his policies.

On the surface it appeared that Venezuela had indeed entered a new and promising era. The administrative ability, the financial acumen, the military stratagems, the political shrewdness, and the rapid initial series of apparent policy successes demonstrated by Guzmán Blanco blinded many concerning the true nature of his régime. Only after he went to Europe in 1877, leaving the country in charge of a puppet ruler, was the veil removed and the tyrant exposed. When the opposition rebelled, Guzmán Blanco returned to crush it and resume the presidency for five more years in 1879. Again in 1886 he returned from Europe, having left another puppet ruler in charge since 1884, to serve a final term of two years in the face of widespread domestic opposition.

Though he proclaimed himself spokesman for the Liberal Party and defender of its principles, Guzmán Blanco possessed neither a political ideology nor party responsibility. His ruthless attacks upon the Conservatives represented personal vengeance, not party principle. He made a sham of political liberalism by rigging elections, muzzling the press, and terrorizing all opposition. The federalism for which the party had long fought was perverted into an autocratic centralism under which Guzmán Blanco himself assumed the role of a vainglorious Caesar.

Eulogistic inscriptions, magnificent statues, and flattering portraits turned all public works projects into monuments to the dictator. Financial reorganization and honesty in government was undertaken primarily to improve Guzmán Blanco's own opportunities for graft. Even before he became President, he had already amassed a sizable fortune by financial chicanery while negotiating foreign loans for the Government. As President, public works contracts and foreign concessions afforded the *caudillo* vast new opportunities for graft.

Similarly, Guzmán Blanco's attacks on the Church stemmed not so much from deep-seated anti-clerical convictions as they did from his desires to deify and magnify himself. He viewed his war on the Church in terms of political opportunity and economic gain for himself. The Catholic Church in Venezuela never fully recovered from the blows he administered. Its wealth and political influence were destroyed, and its spiritual power over the masses of the people was sharply reduced.

Moreover, Guzmán Blanco's initial efforts to foster public education were not sustained. His promotion of material progress was only a peripheral interest. Valuable mineral resources were alienated on terms unfavourable to the nation. The backward agricultural base of the economy was not transformed in any fundamental way. The miserable lot of the masses was not noticeably improved.

In sum, though Guzmán Blanco's rule had positive aspects, on balance his was a régime that brought few lasting benefits to the nation. Once his political power finally came to an end in 1888, subsequent Governments were forced to devote their energies to extricating the country from the old problems he had left unsolved and the new ones he had created.[4]

For a decade after the death of Guzmán Blanco, the Venezuelan state floundered in new political chaos. For four years civilian elements tried to re-establish responsible, representative government. In 1892, the military, led by General Joaquín Crespo, took power by force. Crespo, though he ruled for six years, was not destined to assume Guzmán Blanco's dictatorial mantle for long. Instead this was to pass to *caudillos* from the Andean state of Táchira.

CIPRIANO CASTRO

The end of the century was a turning-point in Venezuelan history. Late in 1899 a band of revolutionaries from the mountain state of Táchira, in the south-west corner of the republic, descended upon Caracas, overwhelmed the regular army, and seized the Government. For the next forty-six years, till the end of the Second World War, *tachirense caudillos* controlled the political scene.

The *llanos* had produced General Páez as the first long-term ruler of the republic, then there successively came to power General Monagas from the humid north-east coast, followed by Marshal Falcón from the arid north-west coast. The late nineteenth century was dominated by Guzmán Blanco, from Caracas. With the coming to power of the *andinos* at the turn of the century, the pattern of political control of the nation by regional *caudillos* had come full circle.

General Cipriano Castro, who ruled Venezuela from 1899 to 1908, was probably the worst of her many dictators. A farmer and a cowboy, he entered politics by recruiting a private army and engaging the federal Government in a series of civil wars. Taking advantage of the prevailing anarchy at the centre, he launched a spectacular 500-mile march through the Andes all the way from the Colombian

[4] The best analysis of this infamous dictator is George S. Wise's *Caudillo: A Portrait of Antonio Guzmán Blanco* (1951).

border to Caracas. He was firmly entrenched in the nation's capital as the twentieth century opened. Castro was despotic, reckless, licentious, and corrupt and his régime was characterized by administrative tyranny, inefficiency, graft and extravagance, by financial chaos, by almost constant domestic revolt, and by frequent foreign interventions.

Soon after the dictator seized power, a major rebellion led by Manuel Antonio Matos broke out in eastern Venezuela. Various regional *caudillos*, fearful of losing their local authority, joined the so-called Liberating Revolution. For more than two years there was heavy fighting. Most of the republic fought the *andinos*, but Castro triumphed in April 1903. Subsequently there were other uprisings, but Castro remained in power, thanks mainly to the able General Juan Vicente Gómez, who was equal to the task of quelling rebellions whenever and wherever they occurred.

Castro's international problems sprang from his cavalier treatment of foreign business men and diplomats. Always in financial straits, due primarily to fiscal mismanagement and extravagance, he attempted to raise funds by fining foreign firms for alleged complicity in revolutionary activities. These tactics, together with Castro's refusal to pay damages resulting from the destruction of foreign properties during the repeated insurrections, led to foreign intervention on a number of occasions.

In 1902 British, German, and Italian warships blockaded Venezuela and bombarded the coastal cities. This action, followed by the appearance of United States warships on the scene, forced Castro to capitulate, but soon after the blockade was lifted, in 1903, he continued to harass foreign businesses. In 1908, after he had dismissed the Netherlands Minister on charges of political intrigue and stopped all trade between Venezuela and the Dutch West Indies, a Dutch squadron appeared off the coast, seized a port, and destroyed a part of Venezuela's small navy.

Castro's downfall, however, resulted neither from his manifold domestic problems nor from foreign action. It was his health and an over-ambitious subordinate that were directly responsible for his political demise. Castro's almost constant dissipation, his overdoses of spirits and aphrodisiacs ended by ruining him physically. In November 1908 he went to Germany in the hope of obtaining a cure for a serious kidney complaint. During his convalescence his trusted associate, General Gómez, was left in charge. Gómez usurped the presidential powers and did not relinquish them until his death twenty-seven years later.

JUAN VICENTE GÓMEZ

Juan Vicente Gómez, like Castro, was a Táchira cowboy and farmer. He was born out of wedlock in 1857, the son of a Spanish immigrant father and an illiterate Indian mother. His mother married a local farmer, Pedro Cornelio Gómez, who brought up Juan together with the nine children of the marriage. On the death of his step-father, Juan, at the age of fourteen, became head of the family, whose fortunes notably improved under his able farm management and shrewd livestock dealings. While thus engaged, he found time to educate himself, learning to read and write and taking an interest in national affairs.

His entry into politics dates from the early 1890's when he became involved in the regionalist uprisings of his neighbour, Cipriano Castro. As Castro's most valued field commander, he was awarded the governorship of the Federal District when the *andino* revolutionaries took Caracas in 1899. Thereafter his brilliant victories against Castro's opponents won him the office of Vice-President in 1904. As soon as Castro left for Europe in 1908, Gómez began replacing the state governors, the men who managed the election of members of the Congress. The latter in turn elected Gómez President in 1910.

Gómez was a mixture of the two races, the Indian and the Spanish, that gave the nation its *mestizo* blend. Similarly his religious beliefs combined Spanish Catholicism with primitive Indian superstition. The vicissitudes of his youth convinced him of the usefulness of shrewdness, force, and cunning in the attainment of power and wealth. He was an uncanny judge of men. He rewarded the loyal, but pursued and punished those whom he distrusted. His relations with women were ephemeral. He fathered more than a hundred children and provided for all of them, but he never married. He lived quietly, alone, in modest surroundings in Maracay. Absolute power and unlimited wealth were his chief aims and values.

Though Gómez was not President continuously, he was always absolute ruler. Sometimes he allowed puppets, like Dr. Victorino Márquez Bustillos (1914–22) and Juan Bautista Pérez (1929–31), to occupy the presidential chair while he continued to exercise supreme authority from his alternate post as Minister of War. Several times the Constitution was changed in response to his whims. By controlling and manipulating elections and by declaring a moratorium on all organized political activity, he obtained a completely subservient legislative and court system.

A key element in the Gómez power structure was the army, which he so thoroughly reorganized, modernized, and expanded that would-be domestic revolutionaries dared not challenge him. One of the first things he did, after shuffling the top army commands so that his Táchira partisans were in all the key posts, was to set up a military academy in Caracas. A Chilean mission was employed to run the school and undertake the reorganization and professionalization of the army. These Chileans, who had been trained by the Germans, introduced the latest European equipment and methods. After the First World War the most promising young army officers were sent to advanced training schools in France and Peru, while French and Italian airmen built up an air force at Maracay. To keep the army loyal, he paid the officers well, and in addition endowed them with special social and legal privileges and with opportunities for self-enrichment.

Moreover, Gómez's public works programme was de-

liberately designed to tighten and make the military dictatorship more all-pervasive. For example, a network of
roads was constructed to enable the army to move promptly
into hitherto isolated parts of the republic. When Gómez's
master control plan was completed, uprisings by regional
caudillos were henceforth out of the question.

In addition to outlawing political parties and muzzling
the press, he sought to eliminate all opposition through an
elaborate spy organization. Paid informers in the army, in
the bureaucracy, in the foreign service, and in the streets
enabled him to hunt down his antagonists. Critics were
silenced by arbitrary arrest and incarceration. In three
major prisons—La Rotunda in Caracas, El Libertador in
Puerto Cabello, and San Carlos on a small island at the entrance to Lake Maracaibo—the opponents of the régime
were clamped in leg irons and subjected to tortures. Hundreds died of thirst, starvation, and disease.

Meanwhile the Government's propaganda machine por-
trayed the régime in a most favourable light both at home
and abroad. And Gómez could boast of some impressive
achievements. In contrast with the general chaos characteristic of the Castro régime, the Gómez Government provided financial order and political tranquillity. Not only
was the interest on the foreign and domestic debt paid off,
but the principal began to be paid too, and all reasonable
claims against the Government were honoured. Whereas
Castro had antagonized foreign investors, Gómez invited
them to come in and develop the republic's national resources upon very favourable terms.

These new conditions enticed petroleum investors in particular, especially after 1911 when Mexico entered an era
of revolution and uncertainty following the collapse of the
Díaz régime. Just before the First World War Gómez's
liberal concessions policy brought in the Royal Dutch-
Shell interests, and immediately after the war a whole group
of United States firms came in to compete with the British
and the Dutch. In 1918 Gómez allowed the companies to

draft the kind of petroleum legislation under which they wished to operate and then decreed it the law of the land. The result of such a benevolent attitude and the presence of vast oil deposits in the Lake Maracaibo basin transformed Venezuela from an insignificant oil producer at the end of the First World War into the world's second producer and leading exporter by 1928.

The economic consequences of petroleum development permeated the whole country. Foreign trade increased rapidly. Direct and indirect government revenues from the petroleum industry accounted for half the Government's total revenues by 1929. The world depression halted expansion only temporarily. By 1935 the 1929 peak had been surpassed and the *llanos* oilfields were beginning to be opened up.

The oil industry brought great benefits to the nation. The companies mapped large areas of national territory and built roads. They employed Venezuelans, improved their health, education, and living conditions, and paid them high wages. Venezuelan commerce prospered from the industry's foreign imports and domestic purchases. During the gradual decline of agricultural exports in the mid-1920's the growing oil industry took up the slack, and it was the continued high level of petroleum exports that saved the economy from collapse during the world depression.

The extraordinary income from oil enabled Gómez to pay off the entire foreign debt and most of the domestic debt by 1930. Petroleum revenues also enabled him to undertake a broad public works programme and grant subsidies to agriculture. In addition to building roads, he promoted expansion of railway and port facilities and was responsible for the construction of a large number of new public buildings.

Rationalization for the close association between the dictatorial Government and foreign investors was supplied by Gómez's semi-official apologist, Laureano Vallenilla Lanz. His book *Cesarismo Democrático*, issued by the Government in 1929, expounded the philosophy of the Gómez régime. According to it, inasmuch as the Venezuelans were a mixed and primitive race living in a backward, pastoral economy, military dictatorship was not a necessary evil but, rather, the best possible form of government. For the strong man really represented the unconscious desire of the people to have demagogues, Communists, and revolutionary adventurers suppressed and order maintained. The nation's benevolent despot, representing the collective will, met the people's desire to improve their lot by arranging for national development to be undertaken by the more advanced, technologically superior, foreigners.

But Gómez did almost nothing to elevate the Venezuelan people. Living standards were miserably low; there was no government housing; health and education were neglected despite the opulence of the state; agriculture and industry were prostrate. It seemed as though the only beneficiaries of the Gómez system, besides the oil firms, were himself, his family, the military officers, and his Táchira friends in high government positions. Gómez ran the nation as the private preserve of his own family and the army. Through various kinds of graft, particularly peculation in dealing in oil concessions, and through confiscating the properties of his opponents, he became the nation's largest landholder. His accumulated fortune in cattle, coffee plantations, industrial plant, and real estate was estimated at over $200 million. His associates enriched themselves with the residue.

Despite the brutality, the terror, the torture chambers, the censorship, and the complete absence of civil liberties, the opposition could not be completely throttled. It was apparent to many Venezuelans that petroleum was not an unmixed blessing. For while oil was developed, agriculture and stockraising declined. As a consequence the country began to lose the capacity to feed itself, and had to import high-cost food. Petroleum 'prosperity' meant rapid price increases, and wages lagged far behind. Worst of all, the opposition stated, oil contributed to the maintenance

49

of a corrupt and brutal dictatorship, for the oil income was all too often used to purchase official sycophants and to improve the efficiency of the instruments of public repression, particularly the army, the police, and the spy system.

Leaders of the opposition were the students at the Central University in Caracas. Ideologically influenced by the First World War, the Mexican revolution of 1910, and the Russian revolution of 1917, it was they who first saw that Gómez was more than a national despot, that he was also the instrument of the foreign control of the Venezuelan economy. For them the battle cries became democracy, economic nationalism, and social justice.

In February 1928 there occurred the first serious challenge to the régime as students began making anti-Government speeches and agitating for relaxation of the dictatorship. The Government responded by arresting the leaders, an action which provoked a nation-wide student strike and brought crowds into the streets. These were dispersed by gunfire, the universities were closed, and the students were rounded up and put to work on the roads. Many of the leaders of this so-called 'generation of 1928' fled the country.

The student uprisings and the popular demonstrations convinced several long-exiled opponents of the Gómez régime that the time was ripe for invasion. In 1929 General Ramón Delgado Chalbaud organized an assault on the north-east coast from Paris. The movement, poorly coordinated, was easily quelled by Gómez's efficient army. Two years later General Rafael Simón Urbina launched an assault on the north-west coast from Curaçao. Since the expected popular uprising did not materialize, this invasion also ended in failure. This was the last serious attempt to overthrow the tyrant. He remained complete master of the political situation till his death, from natural causes, on 17 December 1935, at the age of seventy-nine.

ELEAZAR LÓPEZ CONTRERAS

As the news spread that Gómez had died, the pent-up resentment asserted itself in popular uprisings. Enraged mobs looted or destroyed much of the property of Gómez and his relatives. Rioting and demonstrations in Caracas forced many frightened high government officials to flee into exile. In Maracaibo crowds poured through the streets, sacked business places, burned the looted buildings, massacred Gómez's collaborators, and razed the Foreign Club. At the main oilfields on the east shore of Lake Maracaibo the wives and children of the foreign oil men had to be rushed to safety on lake tankers as rioters threatened to set fire to the wells and storage tanks and demolish the camps.[5] Thus it appeared that popular reaction against the long period of brutal and corrupt tyranny was going to bring sweeping changes to Venezuela—perhaps a social upheaval similar to Mexico's after Díaz was ousted.

Drastic change did not occur, however, for the people were without leaders. The oligarchy for so long associated with the dictator—the generals, the large landholders, and the *gomecista* Congress—moved to preserve order by hastily choosing the Minister of War, General Eleazar López Contreras, as President to serve the remainder of Gómez's term ending in April 1936, when they 'elected' him President for another five years.

López Contreras promptly sent troops to quell the uprisings, replacing the high officials who had fled by less notorious *gomecistas*, and briefly attempted to rule by decree. In the face of widespread demands for the restoration of civil liberties, he realized that his political survival would depend upon relaxation of the dictatorship. Once order was restored, political prisoners were freed; the press was unmuzzled; the opposition came out of hiding; exiles were allowed to return from abroad. In April 1936 a new Constitution was adopted, which reduced the President's term from seven to five years and prohibited immediate re-

[5] E. Lieuwen, *Petroleum in Venezuela* (1954), p. 72.

election. In addition Congress, in the spring of 1936, passed a very advanced labour law, which unequivocally gave labour the right to organize and to affiliate with international bodies, and which provided for profit sharing, social insurance, and an eight-hour working day.

The new freedoms were swiftly taken advantage of by returning student leaders of the 'generation of 1928' and by an assortment of popular politicians and labour organizers representing the new social groups created by the growing cities and oil industry. These new political movements and labour organizations were radical and revolutionary in character. They were determined to dismantle the *gomecista* system, to change the nation's colonial-type economic structure, and to elevate the people both politically and socially.[6]

Petroleum workers' syndicates were rapidly organized at each of the principal oil camps, and though no formal federation was set up, labour leaders established informal ties among local workers. And their work was effective. On 14 December 1936, when the union leaders failed to get satisfaction for various demands from the companies, a general strike was called. To the amazement of both Government and industry, 20,000 workers left their jobs.

Meanwhile in the cities broadly-based political parties began to emerge during 1936. The new leaders expounded the 'people's' cause in the press and at public rallies. The largest popular party was the Venezuelan Organization (ORVE), led by members of the 'generation of 1928' who had just returned from exile. In the congressional election of January 1937 the combined leftist opposition, despite voting restrictions, shocked the López Contreras Government by winning the impressive number of thirty seats.

Although the traditionalist party, the Bolivarian Civic Group (ACB), retained a majority in Congress, these new radical deputies, with their insistent demands for democracy, social justice, and economic liberation, convinced

[6] Rómulo Betancourt, *Venezuela; política y petróleo* (1956), pp. 79–91.

López Contreras that his brief political liberalization experiment would have to end.

A product of the *gomecista* tradition, he was psychologically incapable of accepting a popular opposition or of promoting genuine democracy. He was, after all, a member of the ruling regional military clique. He had been born in Táchira in 1883, had fought alongside Castro and Gómez in the 1899 revolution and, after thirty-five years of loyal support and efficient military service on behalf of the regionalist clique, was the natural choice of those in power to carry on the *gomecista* tradition.

Actually the liberalization that took place in Venezuela in the immediate post-Gómez era was the bare minimum required to still popular pressures. The 1936 Congress, still manned by Gómez's hand-picked deputies and senators, refused to make any fundamental reform in the Constitution. No provision was made for broadening the electoral base—only one-sixteenth of the populace was eligible to vote—and the citizenry continued to be excluded from direct participation in the election of the President and Congressmen. The latter continued to be chosen by state legislatures and municipal councils, while the President was elected by Congress.

Moreover the López Contreras Government soon took back from labour the rights and privileges it had granted under the 1936 law. The December oil strike was interpreted as a strike against the Government as well as the petroleum industry, for when production stopped, so did the Government's royalty payments. It was not long before the paralysis in the country's chief industry was felt throughout the whole economy. In consequence, the patience of the President soon wore thin. On 22 January 1937 he decreed the strike at an end, gave the workers a small pay increase, and ordered them all back to work.

Convinced of the collusion of the organized labour leaders and the leftist political opposition, he proceeded to crush both. Thirty 'labour agitators' were arrested and expelled from the Lake Maracaibo region; the recently organized Trade Union Congress was dissolved. The President justified his action on the grounds that organized labour had strayed from purely economic activities, that personal political ambition—which he would not tolerate—had perverted and corrupted the labour movement. Henceforth labour's welfare would be taken care of exclusively through the paternalistic concern of the President.[7]

To deal with the popular political opposition, a somewhat different tactic was necessary. Taking advantage of broad powers granted him under the 1936 Constitution to curb Communists, terrorists, and anarchists, López Contreras branded forty-seven leftist politicians as 'Communists'. Most of them were exiled; some were imprisoned; a few went into hiding. To make the repression complete, he outlawed ORVE and two smaller leftist parties. For the rest of López Contreras's term of office, until just before the 1940 elections, the President's own party, the ACB, remained the only legal political organization in the country.

With a moratorium thus declared on all opposition political activity, López Contreras devoted his attention to administrative and economic matters. He recognized that the nation was basically backward, that what it needed was a long-range programme of modernization and diversification, a vast improvement in its communications system, and a bettering of the health and educational standards of its people. Such a programme required capital. It could come from only one source—oil. '*Sembrar el petróleo*' was the slogan adopted. The idea was to take the money obtained by the extraction of wealth from Venezuela's soil and 'sow' it in the land in order to establish a healthy diversified economy. During 1936 and 1937 the Government's primary attention was devoted to agriculture. Subsidies to exporters were increased, and crop-expansion and livestock-improvement programmes were launched.

In July 1938 the President inaugurated a broad three-

[7] Lieuwen, *Petroleum*, p. 82.

year programme of material, social, and educational improvement. The plans included railway, highway, port, and airport development projects, the building of houses, schools, hospitals, sewer systems and waterworks, the encouragement of immigration and tourism, the promotion of domestic agriculture and industry, and reduction in the cost of living.

The success of the programme was of course tied to prosperity in the petroleum sector, the principal source of the Government's revenue and axis of the nation's economy. The opening up of new fields in the eastern *llanos* and the expansion of proven areas in the Maracaibo basin increased Venezuela's crude output by over 25 per cent. (from 150 million barrels annually to 200 million barrels annually) during López Contreras's first four years in office. During 1940, however, the adverse effects of the European war (the blockade against the Axis, the German submarine campaign, the tight British control over use of oil tankers) forced a 10 per cent. curtailment of output.

The López Contreras Government passed a new oil law in 1938 which substantially revised operating terms and profit-sharing in favour of the Government, but the companies ignored the new legislation. They applied for no new concessions, and refused to convert or adapt old ones. Instead they continued to operate legally under Gómez's laws. Thus the percentage of the profits the nation received from the industry remained about the same as under Gómez.

How much was actually achieved in material and cultural improvement in the 1936–40 period? The opposition maintained that very little had been done, that little 'sowing the petroleum' was apparent. For when López Contreras's term ended, agriculture was still in the doldrums; there was virtually no increase in employment in domestic industry; government investment in school and hospital construction was, relatively speaking, no greater than under the Gómez régime; transportation and communications facilities were not notably improved; the cost of living rose steeply in the face of the avowed government campaign to lower it; and official graft and corruption were by no means eliminated.

López Contreras maintained that he had made a sound beginning on a difficult long-term problem, that he had drawn up elaborate plans, that he had expanded credit facilities, that he had inaugurated and was well on the way to developing projects in every area of endeavour announced under the three-year plan in 1938. He argued that if these beginnings were not to be fruitless, a man who would carry on his policies would have to be elected.

It was not much of a problem, given the indirect electoral procedures in force in 1940, for López Contreras to hand-pick his successor. The remnants of the ORVE Party had regrouped their forces and organized the Democratic National Party (PDN), but dissension arose between non-Communist and Communist elements, wherepon the latter broke off and organized the Communist Party of Venezuela. It made little difference; both groups were declared 'communistic' and outlawed. Just before the election, the PDN leaders organized the Democratic Action (AD) party. Rómulo Betancourt returned from exile in Chile to direct the AD campaign. The novelist Rómulo Gallegos was AD's candidate for the presidency.

This AD effort to rouse the people and debate the issues was all in vain, however. López Contreras simply ignored the demands of the opposition that the Constitution be changed to permit direct election of the new President. Instead, following the traditional practice, he ordered the state legislatures to elect senators and the municipal councils to elect deputies for the 1941 Congress. As expected, the Government won an overwhelming victory in these late 1940 congressional elections. Then on 28 April 1941 this *lópecista* Congress dutifully elected the successor designated by the then President. The vote was 123 for the Government's candidate, 13 for Gallegos. According to Betancourt:

López Contreras transferred the Government of Venezuela to his own Minister of War, General Isaías Medina Angarita. He thus continued fulfilling in Venezuela, under the norms of an electoral system *sui generis*, the formula . . . whereby the presidency of the republic was the ultimate goal of a military career.[8]

Thus the firm hold the Táchira military established in 1899 was to be continued for yet another term. When Medina was inaugurated, López probably hoped to assume the post of Minister of War again. He obviously planned to return to the presidency in 1946 when Medina's term was due to expire.

ISAÍAS MEDINA ANGARITA

Medina, throughout his entire professional career, had been closely associated with the ruling military clique. He was born in Táchira in 1897, graduated from the Escuela Militar in 1914, and had risen to the rank of colonel by the time of Gómez's death. He had served as López Contreras's right-hand man when the latter was Minister of War in the period 1931–5, and when López Contreras became President, Medina was appointed Minister of War, a post he held until he became President in 1941.

With such a background, it surprised no one when Medina announced his intention of sticking closely to the policies of his predecessor. Soon after taking office he made known his intention of extending and expanding the national development programme inaugurated by López Contreras in 1938. In February 1942 he announced an even more ambitious four-year economic development plan. Emphasis was placed upon modernizing the republic's interior. The numerous projects included the stimulation of agriculture and stock-raising, the improvement of roads and rivers, and the construction of waterworks and sewage facilities in the interior towns and cities.

Before the Government had a chance to implement these plans, however, the nation was forced to brace itself against

[8] Betancourt, p. 127.

57

a sudden economic storm. 1941 had been a good year in the oil industry with a record 228 million barrels produced. Then the bombing of Pearl Harbour brought the war to Venezuela. On the night of 14 February 1942 seven oil tankers, *en route* from Lake Maracaibo to the refineries at Curaçao and Aruba, were torpedoed by German submarines. Though the setting up of a convoy-air patrol system subsequently provided adequate protection, such a severe Allied tanker shortage soon developed that it became impossible to move Venezuela's oil. The result was that production dropped by 25 per cent. in 1942 (down to 148 million barrels), and as a consequence the Government's revenues fell off sharply. During the fiscal year 1942 petroleum taxes and customs receipts, largely dependent on the level of oil industry activity, dropped by more than one-third. In addition, field development came to a halt, causing widespread unemployment.[9]

The impact of the oil industry's depression upon the Venezuelan budget and economy produced widespread popular demands for an increase in the nation's share in the profits of the industry. Medina, a much more astute politician than his predecessor, decided that the moment was opportune to force the companies into accepting a basic revision of the republic's oil legislation. He asked industry's co-operation, then threatened a variety of legal actions when this co-operation was at first refused. Early in 1943 discussions began. Industry's objections to the proposed law were weighed against government demands. A whole series of compromises were hammered out, whereupon the President summoned a special session of Congress to give its approval.

On 13 March 1943 Venezuela passed a new oil law, which unified a whole maze of previous legislation, required the companies to increase their refining capacities in Venezuela, and increased taxes and royalties to the point where the treasury's petroleum revenues were expected to

[9] Lieuwen, *Petroleum*, pp. 90–91.

equal the profits of the industry. In exchange for company promises to convert all old concessions to the new law, Medina agreed to renew all titles for an additional forty years and to drop all pending lawsuits against the industry. The 1943 law was truly a sweeping and long-overdue reform. It was designed to regulate Government–industry relations until at least 1983.[10]

Economic prosperity returned to Venezuela during 1944. As the submarine menace disappeared and the transportation shortage eased, the Allies began making unprecedented demands for oil. In response, the Medina Government granted over 13 million acres of new concessions. During 1945 crude production soared past the 300 million barrels per annum mark. The oil boom in turn stimulated an upsurge in the entire economy.

As a result of the 1943 law, the new concessions, and the increased production, Medina was now provided with the wherewithal to revive his four-year plan. Petroleum revenues poured into the federal coffers so rapidly that they could not be absorbed, and dollar reserves began to accumulate. During 1944 and 1945 construction activity on airports, roads, hospitals, and schools (including a new Central University campus), reached a record level.

However, at the very height of Venezuela's wartime economic boom, the Medina administration was suddenly overthrown with surprising ease. The October 1945 revolution revealed that the régime's notable economic successes had obviously not been matched in the realm of politics.

Medina, it must be admitted, had more flexible political policies than his predecessors. Just as a rapidly changing Venezuelan economy and society made it impossible for López Contreras to continue the Gómez-type despotism, so the acceleration of these social and economic changes during the Second World War forced President Medina to allow additional political freedoms. Besides, Medina's

[10] Ibid. pp. 93–97.

tenure of office coincided with the world-wide struggle of Allied democracy against Fascist totalitarianism. Once Caracas broke diplomatic relations with the Axis, on the last day of 1941, and associated itself with the Allied cause, the continued restrictions on civil liberties in Venezuela became more and more anachronistic.

Medina's first moves in a more liberal direction were his appointments of less conservative cabinet officers, state presidents, and supreme court judges. Next he unmuzzled the press and permitted freedom of association and free speech. All political prisoners were released, and exiles were allowed to return. Opposition parties, regardless of their political colour, were allowed to organize.

In essence, the Medina régime was of a moderate, middle-of-the-road type, and its support came chiefly from middle-class elements in the society. In addition, it had substantial support from the Communists. The rightist opposition rallied around López Contreras, while the labour-leftist majority backed AD.

Actually, President Medina gave up very little in the way of personal power when he restored civil and political liberties, for he retained formidable legal weapons which he did not hesitate to use to stifle opposition threats. Chief of these was the Law of Public Order, first used by López Contreras to throttle the labour leftists in 1937, which was an ever-present threat to radical leaders. In addition, Congress, during 1942, approved Medina's request for the suspension of constitutional guarantees and conferred upon him emergency powers to administer national affairs during the international crisis. Such special powers were really unnecessary, for the organized opposition supported the régime's pro-Allied foreign policy. AD realized the importance of Venezuela's oil to the democratic world cause, and the Communists too, once Russia broke with the Axis, approved Medina's anti-Nazi policies.

What protected the régime's political position in the face of the growing labour-leftist opposition was control of the election machinery and continuance of the indirect methods of voting. Using the former device during 1942 the Government succeeded in electing 286 of its 302 candidates for the state legislative assemblies and 981 out of its 1,405 candidates for municipal councils. Then in January 1943 the state legislatures elected new members to the national Senate, and of course it surprised no one that all the pro-Government candidates won. In the Chamber of Deputies, whose membership was elected by the municipal councils, the régime's control was not nearly so complete, principally because there was far more popular participation in the local elections. The result was that about a third of the new council men were anti-Government, and they in turn elected a vigorous and vociferous anti-Medina minority, most of them AD partisans, to serve in the Chamber of Deputies.

In the face of this rising political strength of the left, Medina decided to combat it by forming an official party, at first called the Partisans of Government Policy, later renamed the Venezuelan Democratic Party (PDV). This party had a very important mission to perform, for out of the 1944 state legislature and municipal council elections would emerge the 1945 Congress, which in turn would elect Medina's successor. By 1945 the President had broken with López Contreras and the rightists, and apparently intended to nominate his own successor and return to the presidency himself in 1951. By hard work at the local level—and by the use of coercion, bribery, and various forms of electoral fraud, according to the opposition—the PDV won an overwhelming victory in the October 1944 elections, and increased its control over the 1945 Congress. Thus it appeared Medina would have little trouble in designating his successor.

The year 1945 was one of intense political activity. It was the year when the war came to an end and thus obliged the President to give up his wartime emergency powers. Medina, though determined that a man sympathetic to his views and pliable to his wishes would succeed him, was

politician enough to realize, however, that the imposition
of an unpopular puppet would make it extremely difficult
to control the opposition.

Accordingly, during 1945, the Government, through the
PDV, conducted a campaign to promote greater popular
support for its policies and began to search for a suitable
successor to Medina. In April the *medinista* Congress approved a whole series of liberal constitutional amendments,
among them being direct election of the Chamber of Deputies, and votes for women in the municipal elections. Then
during the summer the PDV met to select a presidential
candidate. After prolonged discussions and the rejection of
various candidates suggested by the left—and of López
Contreras, as suggested by the right—the PDV decided to
nominate Diógenes Escalante, who was then Venezuelan
Ambassador to Washington. Medina assumed that Escalante, a liberal and a civilian, might be acceptable to the
labour-leftist opposition, as in fact he was. AD was agree-
ably surprised at the choice, and promptly sent two party
representatives to Washington to interview him. Upon receiving assurances from Escalante that he would attempt to
move rapidly in the direction of broad political, social, and
economic reform, AD agreed to support him as a National
Unity candidate.[11]

The traditionalist elements, however, the large landholders, and a number of senior army officers were severely
disturbed. Their candidate was López Contreras, and when
he was publicly rejected by Medina and the PDV in the
summer of 1945, his partisans promptly formed a new
rightist party called Group in Favour of the Presidential
Candidacy of López Contreras. Since the *medinista* Congress was obviously going to nominate someone else, there
was no way for the *lopecistas* to gain power except by force of
arms.

During the summer of 1945 the nation was tense amidst
rumours that the *pax tachirense*, which had enforced political

[11] Betancourt, p. 192.

order ever since the turn of the century, was about to be broken by civil war between the *lopecistas* and *medinistas*. They hurled invectives at each other in the streets, in Congress, and in the press, while plotting was rife among the generals and colonels.

Medina, concentrating his efforts upon the threat from the right and the senior officers, was suddenly and surprisingly overthrown on 18 October 1945 by the left and the junior officers. This revolution marked the end of an era: that of the ascendancy of the army generals and the landed aristocracy which had ruled the nation ever since independence.

Chapter III

RECENT POLITICAL HISTORY, 1945-58

THE OCTOBER REVOLUTION

THE October 1945 revolution was the most fundamental in Venezuela's history. This was no palace-type revolt. It was something more than a contest for power amongst the *caudillos*. In fact it was a broadly-based revolution, the upshot of deep-seated class conflicts, a popular movement that sought to alter drastically the relations among the various social groups. The revolution of 1945 marked the assumption, for the first time, of political power by a party (Democratic Action) which represented the people.

In 1908, the year in which Gómez assumed power, the founder of Democratic Action (AD), Rómulo Betancourt, was born in Guatire in the state of Miranda. His secondary education was obtained at the Liceo in Caracas, where he first came under the influence of the republic's leading social novelist, Rómulo Gallegos. Thereafter he enrolled in the Central University where his outspoken idealism soon made him a student leader. Public protests against the Gómez political tyranny won him and his colleagues little except incarceration, and a subsequent attempt at armed revolt resulted in his exile in April 1928.

Betancourt and other leaders of the 'generation of 1928' were exiled from their country until after Gómez died. During 1936, taking full advantage of López Contreras's temporary relaxation of the dictatorship, it was Rómulo Betancourt who spearheaded the creation of the Venezuelan Organization (ORVE), the nation's first labour-leftist political movement. When he was stopped by General López's 1937 repressions he went into hiding, and during the years 1937-9 created a clandestine political reform group which was the nucleus of the AD party. While underground Betancourt wrote critical articles which for a time appeared in the opposition press and, after the press was muzzled, in hand-bills. During 1939 and 1940 he lived in Chile, where he continued his political writings, returning to Venezuela only at the end of López's term, not in time to organize an opposition movement that might seriously contest the election of General Medina as President.

After AD was finally legalized in September 1941, the party grew steadily in size and in momentum to the point where the Medina régime was finally overwhelmed by it. Betancourt and his party organizers spent the Second World War years travelling throughout the interior of the country. To the pauperized rural masses they held out hope of an escape, through political action, from their traditional miseries and frustrations. To the oilfield workers, to the factory wage-owners in the cities, to the office workers, to the shop-keepers, and to the teachers they held out promises of a much better life under AD leadership. After four years of hard work the directors of the national organization could boast of disciplined subordinate bodies in nearly every district and municipality in the republic. The increasingly familiar party line—electoral reform, representative government, administrative integrity, public welfare measures, taxes upon the foreign investors and wealthy Venezuelans —was hammered home at mass party rallies and by the newly founded AD newspaper, *El País*.

To such public criticism no régime had hitherto been subjected in all Venezuela's history. In response to it, President Medina instituted a number of genuine reforms, but in the opinion of AD these always fell far short of the desired mark.

For example AD congressmen condemned Medina's 1943 oil law as hopelessly inadequate. They maintained that the royalty and tax clauses, designed to give the Government a profit share equal to that of industry, were based on unsound calculations. They objected to the use of the 1937–9 period of low market prices as a basis for fixing

65

payments on the grounds that the companies would obtain five-sixths of the profits realized from any increase in crude oil quotations above the low-priced 1937–9 base period. The only way to make equal participation in profits effective, they maintained, was to levy a flexible tax which could be assessed on company earnings at the end of each year.[1]

AD was equally critical of the manner in which Medina spent the petroleum income. They maintained that there was widespread corruption and maladministration in official circles, that the benefits of the industry were not filtering down to the people. They charged that, despite the greatly increased income from petroleum, the education budget was not appreciably increased, that no new schools were being built, that illiteracy was increasing; also, that the nation's health was being neglected, that disease was widespread, that mortality rates were unnecessarily high, that there were too few hospitals and doctors to serve the needs of the people. They pointed out that practically nothing had been done by the Government to stimulate agriculture and domestic industry.

AD also maintained that the Medina régime, like its predecessor, was little more than government by and for the army officers, the bankers, and landed oligarchy, and that under it the rich became richer, the poor poorer. They wanted to know why the Government refused to tackle the urgent problem of agrarian reform, why they neglected to adjust salaries to rapid wartime increases in the cost of living.

In addition, AD pointed out that the Government's true attitude towards the Venezuelan people was revealed by the cavalier manner in which Medina dealt with organized labour. At first Medina had been disposed to allow labour much greater freedom than had his predecessor. However, when industry–labour disputes arose, AD complained that the President was too quick to make use of his wartime emergency powers to put an end to them by executive de-

[1] Lieuwen, *Petroleum*, pp. 100–1.

cree. As AD gained a position of increasing dominance over the whole organized labour movement, the latter began to find itself under attack for engaging in 'political' activities. In March 1944 Medina decreed the dissolution of the National Labour Convention and all ninety-three of its affiliated unions, declaring that there had been 'political adulteration of the syndicalist movement'.[2] When new petroleum unions formed and they threatened to strike for higher wages in November 1944, Medina resolved the matter in a manner wholly unsatisfactory to labour by decreeing a 2-bolivar-per-day increase. The administration's belated and partial reform of the 1936 labour law in May of 1945 was denounced as completely inadequate.[3]

From the time of its founding, AD had demanded electoral reform. The misuse of the secret ballot, the prevalence of electoral fraud, the restriction of the franchise, and the indirect methods of electing congressmen and the President all combined to enable the régime in power to win overwhelming victories in elections despite the fact that a large majority of the people opposed it. Inasmuch as AD's continuing demands for direct, universal, and secret suffrage were ignored by Medina's Venezuelan Democratic Party (PDV), which continued the traditional electoral manipulation to gain the results desired by the régime in municipal, state, and congressional elections in 1942, 1943, and 1944, there seemed no way for AD to gain power short of revolution.

A ray of hope appeared, as already indicated, when Medina, in September 1945, agreed to support Diógenes Escalante as a compromise unity candidate to succeed him, for AD had faith in Escalante's promises to introduce electoral reforms, and accordingly they agreed to support his candidacy. However, Escalante suddenly became ill, suffered a nervous breakdown, and withdrew just two months before the scheduled elections of a new President and Congress.

[2] Ibid. pp. 101–2.   [3] Ibid.

Medina then called a convention of the PDV, which on
1 October dutifully selected Angel Biaggini as substitute
candidate. Biaggini, the Minister of Agriculture, was an obscure and colourless political figure. It was obvious to all
that he would be nothing more than a puppet President, a
figurehead for Medina, who planned to continue ruling
from behind the scenes. Accordingly AD refused to back
him. Instead they appealed to Medina to consult with all
the important political groups so as to select a neutral person to serve as provisional President for one year, during
which time the Constitution might be amended to provide
for the election of a President by direct, universal, and secret
suffrage. When this novel idea was summarily rejected by
Medina, the last peaceful and legal avenue to political
power was closed to AD. Their only remaining one was
through violence.[4] An opportunity to make use of such
methods had been offered AD by disgruntled young army
officers four months previously. They now decided to accept
that offer.

Opposition to the administration by the junior officers in
the armed forces had been growing ever since the outbreak
of the Second World War. After Gómez died, the army, like
the people, anticipated great changes. The young officers
expected that the old *gomecista* generals would now be
forced to retire, thus paving the way for military reforms
(particularly modernization of training and equipment)
and rapid promotions. Instead the superannuated, traditionalist, *gomecista* generals maintained their dominant
military and political positions, first under López, then
under Medina, and gave no indication of any intention to
relax their grip. As a consequence, salaries of junior officers
remained low and were not adjusted sufficiently to compensate for the rapid wartime increases in the cost of living.
Moreover, promotions were extremely slow, and the *gomecista* generals showed no interest in applying the new techniques, ideas, and equipment the young officers were learn-

[4] Betancourt, p. 195.

ing about at the Escuela Militar and at advanced training schools in the United States. Instead the complacent senior officers seemed content to allow the armed forces to stagnate while they continued to feather their own nests through the age-old methods of official graft and peculation.

A number of idealistic young officers also became increasingly aware of the popular pressures that were building up against the Medina régime. They began to fear that unless the traditional pattern of senior army officers running the Venezuelan Government as their personal political and economic domain were altered, a violent popular civilian uprising might ultimately break out and destroy the army. Thus some of the young officers, in the face of the apparently irresponsible attitude of the generals, felt impelled to act on behalf of the people.

For a variety of reasons, then, varying from personal ambition to a high sense of national duty and responsibility, a restless group of junior officers formed the Patriotic Military Union (UPM) during 1944. It was a conspiratorial organization created for the purpose of overthrowing the Medina régime. Its stated aims were to put an end to corrupt and incompetent government, to introduce political responsibility, universal suffrage and constitutional reform, and to create a truly professional, a-political army. The members of UPM declared in their charter that they had no personal or class interests to defend, and they sought to prove this by forming an alliance with the political party with aims most similar to theirs. They chose AD.[5]

Accordingly in June 1945 the directors of the UPM sent word to Rómulo Betancourt that they would like to speak with him. The AD leader consulted with party leaders, and a meeting was arranged for 6 July. Here Major Marcos Pérez Jiménez, spokesman for the UPM, told the AD leaders that a coup was being planned, invited AD to join the uprising, and requested Betancourt to take charge of the new Government.

[5] Ibid. pp. 189–90.

Understandably AD leaders were surprised. They had been unaware of the widespread opposition to Medina inside the armed forces. They were also embarrassed by the proposals, for they had missed few opportunities publicly to denounce army intervention into politics. During August and September AD continued to hold discussions with the UPM, during which time they became convinced of the military conspirators' disinterested intentions and of their determination to act whether AD joined them or not. When Medina, on 1 October, made his arbitrary selection of Biaggini to succeed as President, AD finally decided to cooperate with the UPM.[6]

The insurrection was planned for December, but when the Government got wind of it the conspirators were forced to move two months ahead of schedule. On the night of 17 October AD held a mass rally. On the morning of the 18th insurgent young officers took command of the Escuela Militar and seized the Miraflores Presidential Palace and barracks. By noon AD party militants and rebel troops were battling with police and loyal troops in the centre of Caracas. By nightfall the issue was decided. Medina was forced to resign and both he and López Contreras, along with their associates, were arrested and ordered to go into exile. On the 19th Rómulo Betancourt selected a seven-man junta. Only two wore uniforms—Majors Mario Vargas and Carlos Delgado Chalbaud. Besides Betancourt three AD party leaders were selected, and the seventh member was an independent. The Caracas junta promptly extended its control, without too much difficulty, to the interior barracks and cities. Total casualties numbered about 2,500.

THE ACCIÓN DEMOCRÁTICA GOVERNMENT

True to their word, the young officers initially cooperated in establishing a broadly-based civilian Government. They limited their role to maintaining order and seeing to it that the AD programme was carried out. The task

[6] Betancourt, pp. 186–95.

of directing the difficult transition of the republic from its customary rule by the oligarchy and the Táchira military clique to representative democracy was largely in the hands of the Provisional President, Betancourt. Also head of the AD party, he governed for over two years by decree. Hundreds of directives were drawn up by AD's National Executive Committee, then issued by Betancourt from the presidential palace at Miraflores.

The first matter to be tackled was political reform. Lest anyone should doubt that the revolutionary Government was anything more than provisional or that its leaders had purely personal political motives, the junta promised to hold free elections as soon as possible, to draw up a new Constitution, and to transfer power to a duly elected Government. One of Betancourt's first decrees prohibited any member of the junta from becoming a presidential candidate.

On 15 March 1946 the new electoral law went into effect. It was by far the most democratic in the republic's history. Previous voting restrictions on women and illiterates were removed. Suffrage rights were granted to every Venezuelan over eighteen save criminals and persons in active military service. To accommodate illiterates each voter was to receive an envelope containing pieces of paper of various colours, each colour denoting one of the parties. The law specified that any party might nominate candidates for office and that legislative representation would be apportioned in accordance with the percentage of the total vote each received.

On the same day the junta lifted all checks on constitutional rights. In the new atmosphere of free speech, press, and assembly, five major parties were soon in the field to contest elections to the Constituent Assembly scheduled for October 1946. AD's leading competitor was the Independent Committee for Political and Electoral Organization (COPEI). This was a party of the Christian socialist type. Its strength and leadership came from Catholic laymen, particularly from middle-group elements. Its origins went back to 1936 when Rafael Caldera led a small conservative schismatic group, associated with Andean landholders and the Spanish Falange, in opposition to the López Contreras régime. During the Second World War Caldera was politically inactive, but after the October 1945 revolution he served as Attorney-General for the junta. He formally founded COPEI in 1946 and attempted to broaden the party's base by combining a religious appeal with a moderate social-welfare programme for the lower and middle-income groups. Many former *lopecistas*, for lack of any more conservative party to join, also supported the COPEI.

A third party was the Republican Democratic Union (URD) headed by Jovito Villalba, former student leader of the 'generation of 1928'. In ideology and general programme URD was much like AD. It was perhaps a trifle less left of centre than AD, for its membership and direction were predominantly middle class (professional, commercial, industrial, and student groups), though like AD, it also catered for the labour vote. It attracted many former supporters of Medina's PDV, which had become defunct following the 1945 revolution.

Finally, there were the Communists. They had been active in Venezuela since the 1920's. In March 1931 student leaders of the 'generation of 1928' founded the Communist Party of Venezuela. Gómez soon outlawed the party, but its leaders re-emerged in the ORVE party in 1936. However, as previously indicated, opposition within ORVE from non-Communist elements led to the re-creation, clandestinely, of the Communist Party of Venezuela in 1937. Medina legalized the party, which took the name Popular Union (UP) in 1941. During the Second World War the UP vied with AD and the PDV for control of the organized labour movement, often with marked success. The irreconcilable ambitions of UP's two principal leaders, Gustavo

Machado and Juan Batista Fuenmayor, produced a schism. Fuenmayor withdrew and formed the Unitarian Communist Party (PCU). The latter became known as the 'red' Communists because of the electoral colour assigned it, and for similar reasons Machado's UP wing became known as the 'black' Communists.[7]

Following a spirited six-months' campaign, the October 1946 elections for 160 delegates to the Constituent Assembly took place. An unprecedented number of 1,385,000 persons went to the polls. There was no violence or bloodshed. It was probably the most orderly—and the fairest—election the nation ever experienced.

AD won by a landslide, polling three times as many votes as all the other parties combined. It had had solid support in every state in the nation, and carried every one but Táchira. The latter was won by COPEI, whose strength was concentrated in the Andean states in the west. URD's principal support, on the other hand, came from the northeastern towns and cities along the Caribbean coast. The Communist votes came primarily from Caracas and the Lake Maracaibo petroleum area. The official results were:

Party	No. of Votes	No. of Delegates
AD	1,100,000	137
COPEI	180,000	19
URD	54,000	2
Communists	51,000	2

Source: New York Times, 30 Oct. 1946.

With this overwhelming majority, the AD delegates had no trouble in framing the kind of Constitution the party wanted. After several months' discussion, the new Constitution (Venezuela's twenty-second) became law on 5 July 1947, and the 1936 Constitution, as amended in April 1945, was thereby abrogated.

[7] Robert S. Alexander, *Communism in Latin America* (New Brunswick, N.J., 1957), pp. 253–69.

73

The preamble to the 1947 Constitution[8] stated its key aims as follows:

1. The harmony, the well-being, and the social and individual security of Venezuela and of all who live in its territory and under its law.

2. The affirmation of appropriate nationality, supported in accordance with fraternal co-operation in the concert of nations, in projects of peace and of progress, and with mutual respect of sovereignty.

3. The support of democracy as the only and irrenouncable system of governing its internal conduct and pacific collaboration in the design of promoting that same system in the government and relations of all peoples of the earth.

Clearly reflecting AD's debt to organized labour, the Constitution provided such specific guarantees as the right to work, to organize, to strike, to receive pensions, vacation pay, sick pay, severance pay, plus a share in the profits. In addition, the state assumed responsibility for providing reasonably priced homes for the workers as well as adequate educational and health facilities.[9] The state was awarded a key role in planning and developing the national economy, but the rights of private property were recognized and guaranteed protection.

It was stipulated that the President was to be elected for a four-year term by direct, universal suffrage and that he might not be re-elected for eight years. Provision was made for the customary two-house Congress, now to be elected by direct vote also, and for a Supreme Court to pronounce on the constitutionality of laws.

Despite AD's repeated accusations of extreme centralism and excessive executive power in the Medina administration, they did little to change this, for under the 1947 Constitution the President still appointed the state governors, and he was authorized to order preventive detention of all

[8] R. H. Fitzgibbon, ed. *The Constitutions of the Americas* (Chicago U.P., 1948).
[9] Arts. 53–61.

persons he believed to be planning to overthrow the Government.

Once the Constitution had been framed, the next step was to elect a new President and a Congress to take over from the provisional junta. In the autumn of 1947 an open, spirited campaign took place. AD's candidate was Rómulo Gallegos, the leading novelist, a former Congressman who had been AD's unsuccessful opponent of Medina in the 1941 elections. Gallegos was a *caraqueño*. He had taught and administered for many years in the secondary schools, had written many novels (the most famous of which was *Doña Barbara*), had been in political exile in Spain during the last five years of the Gómez era, had served briefly as Minister of Education under López Contreras, and then became an opposition Congressman. By 1947, at the age of sixty-three, he had become AD's elder statesman. Gallegos campaigned for state-sponsored industrial and agricultural development, for better roads, for more public works, for less illiteracy, for better health facilities, and for more benefits for labour. He condemned the Communists as undemocratic, labelling them as agents of Russian imperialism. Concerning COPEI, he gave warning against Falangism and sinister Jesuit influences.

Gallegos's chief competitor was COPEI's Rafael Caldera. He too promised more benefits for labour. 'The rich should be less rich, the poor less poor', he said. He pledged that under a COPEI régime, social peace would reign instead of a class struggle which was being provoked by the Marxist philosophy of AD. He condemned AD's atheism and called for a concordat with the Vatican which would abolish the Government's control over Church appointments.

The Communist candidate was Gustavo Machado, who was highly critical of the AD's policies in general and its 'exclusiveness' in particular. The URD did not contest the presidency but ran a full slate of candidates for Congress.

On 14 December 1947 the elections, managed by the

non-partisan Supreme Electoral Council, were held. For the first time Venezuelans were permitted to vote directly for a President and Congressmen. Foreign observers proclaimed the elections as honest and fair. The results for President were:

Gallegos	871,752
Caldera	262,204
Machado	36,514

Party strength in the new Congress was apportioned as follows:

Party	Senate	Chamber of Deputies
AD	38	83
COPEI	4	21
URD	1	4
Communists	1	3

Source: *New York Times*, 16 Dec. 1947.

On 15 February 1948 the duly elected AD constitutional Government was inaugurated, and the junta ceased to exist.

During the twenty-eight months in which political reform and the transition to constitutional Government were being made, Rómulo Betancourt and the junta were also busy implementing other components of AD's revolutionary programme. The first item on the agenda was a drastic revision in petroleum policy. AD deputies had argued, in opposition to the 1943 law, that the tax schedule was not flexible enough to assure the nation a 50 per cent. share in the profits of the industry. And they were right, for as crude prices rose after 1943, the Government's relative share decreased, even though total revenues from industry increased substantially. To balance the income of Government and industry the junta, on the last day of 1945, decreed an extraordinary tax of $27 million on company profits. It then proceeded to provide for a permanent '50-50' division by adding the following clause to the 1942 income-tax law: 'In no case will the companies be able to receive annual profits

76

greater than those received by the Venezuelan Government.'[10]

In addition to increasing its share of company profits, the Government sought to obtain a still larger income by entering the oil business itself. The initial move in this direction was made in June 1947, when the Venezuelan Government for the first time exercised the legal option of receiving part of its royalty in kind instead of in cash. It then exploited the post-war seller's market for crude by obtaining somewhat higher prices from European and Latin American consumers than the companies operating inside Venezuela would have paid in royalties. Then in March 1948 the new Gallegos Government appointed a commission to draw up plans for building a national refinery and decided to look into the possibility of creating a state oil company to exploit the National Reserve fields.[11]

In line with its conservation policy, AD refused to grant any new concessions and insisted that the companies should salvage more natural gas, improve the efficiency of their operations, and eliminate waste. In addition, AD insisted that the companies must assume broader responsibilities toward the Venezuelan nation, that they must contribute to economic development by investing in domestic industry and agriculture as well as purely extractive industry, and that they must do more refining in Venezuela.

AD's aggressive oil policy did not seriously interfere with the expansion of the petroleum industry. In the immediate post-war era, demand and prices were higher than ever, and the Venezuelan operators responded by breaking new production records nearly every week. Between 1945 and 1948 the average annual rate of increase was over 50 million barrels, and in 1948 490 million barrels were produced, two and a half times the pre-war record. This booming pro-

[10] Venezuela, *Gaceta oficial*, 1 Dec. 1946. Venezuela's '50–50' arrangement had world-wide repercussions. Similar 'agreements' were soon forced upon the oil companies by the Governments of Saudi Arabia, Iraq, Kuwait, Qatar, and Bahrain Island.

[11] Lieuwen, *Petroleum*, pp. 106–7.

duction, coupled with the high market prices and the new taxes, enormously increased the Government's income. During 1948 petroleum revenues alone totalled over $400 million, more than double the Government's entire income during Medina's last year in office.[12]

With regard to 'sowing the petroleum' income, AD clearly defined its policy. It argued that since oil taxes constituted payment for extraction of the country's natural wealth, all this income had to be ploughed back into the economy in such a way that new wealth would be produced to replace the assets withdrawn. Thus the Government's unprecedented petroleum income was reinvested, in accordance with a broad, detailed plan, to develop the nation's human and material resources.

Less than two weeks after the October 1945 revolution, Betancourt declared in a public address:

We will make the defence of our human resources the centre of our preoccupation. We will not construct ostentatious skyscrapers, but men, women, and children will eat more, will pay less for clothing and rent, will have better public services, and will be provided with more schools.[13]

According to AD, general living conditions were deplorable in 1945. The mass of the people were undernourished, underpaid, and poorly housed. To remedy this, an emergency programme was launched, aimed at providing full employment, higher salaries, and adequate food. AD's technique was to make private industry and business bear as much of the expense as possible.

To this end, the junta, only five days after the revolution, established a separate Ministry of Labour to carry out a new policy of 'social justice and better conditions for the workers'.[14] Trade unionism was encouraged among all Venezuelan labourers, agricultural and industrial alike. During 1946 over 500 new local unions and 13 national fed-

---

[12] Lieuwen, *Petroleum*, p. 108.   [13] Betancourt, pp. 293–4.
[14] *Gaceta oficial*, 23 Oct. 1945.

erations were formed. The following year the Venezuelan Confederation of Labour was founded, and it promptly became the key political prop of the AD Government.

The manner in which the Government and the unions combined against business to achieve their ends was well illustrated by events in the petroleum industry. Very soon after the new local unions had been organized, the Petroleum Workers' Federation demanded an extensive revision of working conditions. When the companies refused and the workers threatened to strike, the AD Minister of Labour, Raúl Leoni, summoned company and union officials and got them to agree to negotiate, with the Government acting as arbiter in case of a deadlock. During the negotiations the junta made no secret of its sympathy for the workers and guided the talks, step by step, towards a great victory for the employees. Clearly government intervention in industrial disputes was intervention on behalf of labour.

An eighteen-month collective contract regulating conditions of work in the whole petroleum industry was signed on 14 June 1946. It included substantial wage increases, payment for a weekly rest day and for travel time, special compensation for night work, and additional hospital benefits. And when this contract expired at the end of 1947, the AD junta again took a hand and guided discussions towards agreement on a new three-year collective contract, which embodied extensive additional gains for the worker.

Though the petroleum workers, the *élite* of Venezuelan labour, fared better than others, all organized labour benefited greatly under the AD Government. Average wages rose from 7·5 bolivars per day in 1945 to 15 bolivars in 1948.[15] Adjusting for the 30 per cent. increase in the cost of living during this period, real wages rose by 65 per cent. Expenditure of a large part of this additional new income upon prime necessities was reflected in a sixfold increase in food imports and a 50 per cent. rise in textile imports between 1945 and 1948. By subsidizing producers and fixing

[15] Banco Central, *Memoria, 1948*, p. 20.

prices, thus stimulating domestic production of meat, fish, and milk, the Government further helped reduce the dietary deficiencies of the people.

Before the advent of AD, Governments in Venezuela had assumed almost no responsibility for the health of the citizenry. The widespread poverty and undernourishment, the maldistribution of wealth, the shortage of doctors and hospitals, and the tropical climate had combined to produce disease and inordinately high mortality rates. AD was determined to change all this. Protection of the nation's health, they believed, was the responsibility of the state. Accordingly, a vigorous ten-year programme was launched to resolve the problem. The Ministry of Health's budget was quadrupled within three years. The public health campaign centred in the rural areas where conditions were worst. Doctors were sent into the interior to provide medical services to those hitherto ignored. To combat the most deadly diseases, the intestinal ones, sanitary engineering programmes (sewers, waterworks, &c.) received high priority.

AD's anti-malaria campaign produced the most spectacular results. Until 1945 nearly a fifth of the population contracted malaria annually. The AD junta spent 10 million bolivars on DDT insecticides and sprayed all the dwellings in infected areas. By the end of 1947 the age-old malaria scourge had been conquered.

Additional features of AD's public health programme were new hospital construction (100 million bolivars in three years), better hospital equipment, and state-sponsored training of more doctors, nurses, and laboratory technicians.

In addition, the junta launched a housing programme throughout the country by greatly expanding credits to the Workers' Bank. Rural zones, where most dwellings had mud floors and thatched roofs and lacked baths and running water, received top priority. Thousands of modern masonry units were constructed in the countryside, while large multiple dwellings began to replace the shanty-town sections of the major cities.

Educational improvement was also accepted as a state responsibility. Venezuela's late nineteenth-century start in public education under Guzmán Blanco had been brought to a virtual halt under Gómez, and the Governments of López and Medina did little to improve the situation. Accordingly, the AD junta was faced with a situation in which only one-third of the children of school age were attending class and over half the adult population was illiterate. It promptly adopted an aggressive public education policy. Over a period of three years the education budget trebled, and the number of schools and teachers was increased to the point where the primary school enrolment more than trebled (to 500,000) and the secondary and university enrolments more than doubled. In addition, the illiteracy problem began to be combated by the establishment of hundreds of reading and writing centres where, by 1948, over 30,000 adults were enrolled.

Finally, AD introduced into the public education system, by means of newly trained teachers and government propaganda materials, dynamic new educational doctrines. The party was determined to make youth aware of the nation's social realities, its economic dilemmas, and its political difficulties. It strove to encourage creative thinking and activity and to make the younger generation aware that it must lead the republic into the modern world. All this, AD believed, was necessary to pave the way for true democracy.[16]

In the economic realm AD's programme was equally radical and revolutionary. It was determined to transform the existing semi-colonial type economy under which crude oil was exchanged abroad for foodstuffs and manufactured goods, into a diversified, independent economy. AD openly condemned *laissez-faire* economics, insisting instead that

[16] See Betancourt, chs. xii and xiii, for a fuller discussion of AD's public health and public education programmes.

widespread governmental intervention was necessary to attain economic well-being and social security for the Venezuelan people.

Convinced that the existing economy was shamefully lopsided and deformed, the AD junta took prompt action to repair it. In May 1946 it established the Venezuelan Development Corporation (VDC) to increase agricultural production, to develop new industries and improve old ones.

The VDC became the state's central economic planning agency, the official organization for 'sowing the petroleum'. Its aim was to reduce drastically Venezuela's chronic deficit in the production of consumer goods, principally foodstuffs and clothing. Its methods were to extend liberal credits to private business engaged in the production of essential articles and to set up state corporations in those fields where private investors were reluctant to go. Five per cent. of the Government's annual income was set aside to finance the manifold operations of the VDC.

The VDC's main attention went to agricultural development. The food deficit problem was attacked first. Individual farmers and interested corporate producers were made twenty-year loans (at 4 per cent. interest) to purchase the machinery, fertilizer, and seed incidental to expanding the production of maize, rice, beans, and sugar. Success was most spectacular in the last crop. By 1948 newly created corporate domestic producers had nearly halved Venezuela's 1945 sugar import requirements.

The VDC also took vigorous action to resurrect the nation's livestock industry. Liberal credits were extended to import new breeds, to drill water wells, and to combat diseases and insect pests. Though some recovery was evident by 1948, it would take Venezuela many years to become self-sufficient in beef production. The VDC also extended credits to milk producers, but when little immediate expansion in output occurred, the state itself entered the milk-producing, pasteurizing, and distributing business.

Other major aspects of AD's agricultural programme included mechanization, irrigation, and immigration. Rapid mechanization was viewed as the most promising solution to the twin problems of food deficit and shortage of agricultural labour. Accordingly AD encouraged the importation of tractors, modern farm implements, and machinery and opened up a special school in Maracay to train farm-equipment operators. Between 1945 and 1948 tractor imports and machine cultivated areas both quadrupled.[17]

To expand the area of cultivation and increase the productivity of the land, AD launched a number of irrigation projects in the northern half of the country. Into the new farming areas thus created, the Government invited European immigrants, particularly Second World War refugees. Five thousand came in 1946, 11,000 in 1947, and more than 20,000 in 1948.

Yet all these measures did not tackle the fundamental problem—the prevalence of latifundia, the near monopolization of the good arable lands by a small number of landholders, resulting in vast arable areas lying idle and the great mass of the rural population remaining propertyless and pauperized. At the time of the October 1945 revolution 5 per cent. of property holders owned 78 per cent. of the land, and only 10 per cent. of the agricultural families owned any land at all. At the same time less than one-fourth of the arable land was then under cultivation.

AD was thus forced to the hard conclusion that without land redistribution its whole programme for agricultural development must fail. It accordingly decided to undertake what was perhaps its most drastic and fundamental revolutionary action of all, namely agrarian reform. AD's aim was to put the land into the hands of those who would make it productive. It moved slowly and cautiously. First it parcelled out the public lands, then it explained to the large landholders that expropriation would not occur on rationally used lands, and that all expropriation would be ac-

[17] Banco Central, *Memoria, 1949.*

companied by fair and just indemnities to the owners. AD explained that it was not embarking upon agrarian reform for the purpose of punishing the large landowners. Rather it was acting from the economic necessity to increase production and from the social necessity to improve the living conditions of the rural population.

The 1948 Congress framed the Agrarian Reform Law. It was signed by President Rómulo Gallegos on 18 October 1948, the third anniversary of the revolution. To implement this basic reform, the law created a National Agrarian Institute, which was supported by 3 per cent. of the government budget. The Institute's major task was to expropriate idle or unwisely used lands of over 300 hectares, to make just compensation to the owners, and to redistribute these lands in the manner best suited to the promotion of the nation's agricultural development.[18]

Though AD laid emphasis on agricultural development, industry was by no means neglected. AD believed that the nation ought to produce everything possible domestically rather than continue unlimited imports of manufactures. Again the VDC provided the stimulus by granting liberal credits to private businesses and by establishing state corporations in certain economic sectors where private investors could not, or would not, do the job. In the latter category were power development and a national steel industry. By 1948 VDC plants had increased electrical output by nearly 50 per cent. over 1945, but steel remained in the planning stage. VDC loans and technical assistance to private concerns led, by the end of 1948, to substantial increases in the manufacture of processed foods, textiles, clothing, shoes, canned fish and chemical fertilizers. In the

[18] Art. 69 of the 1947 Constitution specified that 'The State will undertake a planned and systematic program, oriented to transform the national agrarian structure, to systematize agricultural and stockraising development, to organize and distribute credit, to improve living conditions in the rural medium and the progressive economic and social emancipation of the peasant population. A special law will determine technical and other conditions. . .'. The October 1948 Agrarian Reform Law was designed to carry out this constitutional mandate.

three-year AD era, Venezuela's industrial production nearly doubled.

Co-ordinated with AD's agricultural and industrial pro-gramme was a project for the basic overhaul of the out-moded and inadequate communications network. Em-phasis here was placed upon road building—repairing and paving existing roads and building new ones in hitherto iso-lated regions. A new rapid-transit *autopista* (freeway) from Caracas to La Guaira was begun in August 1947. AD sought to improve air transport by nationalizing all existing airports and building fifty additional state-owned airports. The state-owned Línea Aeropostal Venezolana, the princi-pal airline, was expanded and modernized to a point where it could compete successfully with the major international companies serving Venezuela. But Rómulo Betancourt took most pride of all in AD's building of a national merchant marine. It completely reorganized the listless state-owned Compañía Venezolana de Navigación, financed the con-struction of new vessels, then joined with Colombia and Ecuador in the formation of the Flota Mercante Gran-colombiana, a corporation designed to pool, for the sake of greater efficiency and economic independence, the ship-ping resources of the three participating nations. By 1948 AD hailed the experiment as a complete success and made ambitious plans to expand the fleet.[19]

THE 1948 COUNTER-REVOLUTION

The sweeping and fundamental nature of AD's pro-gramme of reform, the party leader's impetuous determina-tion to transform the Government almost overnight into a vehicle to satisfy the rising expectations of the hitherto ig-nored lower and middle-income groups in the society, the hasty insistence that civilian democracy must immediately replace the age-old tradition of military rule—all this

[19] Betancourt, pp. 370–6. For the foregoing description of AD's agricul-tural, industrial, and communications programme the author is princi-pally indebted to the above work. See espec. chs. vii–xi.

served to swell the ranks of the opposition. The critics complained that the Government was trying to do too much, and go too far, too fast.

Understandably, the traditionalist elements had little sympathy for the party that had forcefully displaced them. They might have ultimately resigned themselves to the loss of political power had not AD promptly followed up the October 1945 coup with a bold assault upon their wealth and property as well. Soon after assuming power, Rómulo Betancourt issued a decree freezing the bank accounts and blocking the disposal of property of former high administrative officials. Then during 1946 a special Tribunal of Civil and Administrative Responsibility was convened to investigate 150 prominent former officials charged with defrauding the Government through illicit self-enrichment while in office. After a nine-month trial, in which nearly all the accused were convicted, AD confiscated property and holdings to the value of $120 million. Hardest hit were the old *gomecistas*, but office holders of the 1935–45 decade also suffered. Ex-Presidents López Contreras and Medina, for example, were each ordered to surrender about $4 million to the state.[20] These punitive measures were followed by a thorough house-cleaning of the federal bureaucracy. Sinecures were eliminated, incompetent persons were removed, and war was declared on all forms of graft and misuse of public funds.

Drastic as AD's administrative reforms were, those of the economic and social variety alienated ever larger groups of people. Venezuelan merchants and manufacturers, as well as the foreign oil companies, saw their labour costs mount alarmingly as a result of AD's encouragement of trade unionism and its pro-labour policies. Even more hard hit were the large agriculturists, under increasing pressure from AD-backed farm-labour unions. The Agrarian Re-

[20] The entire $12 million fortune of the Gómez-related Pimental family was confiscated. See Venezuela, Junta Revolucionaria de Gobierno, *Recapilación de sentencias . . . por el Jurado de Reponsibilidad Civil y Administrativa* (Caracas, 1946).

form Law flung nearly the entire landholding class into vehement opposition. In addition, AD's revolutionary new educational doctrines were condemned as 'sectarian' by the traditionalist elements, particularly by the Church hierarchy.

And despite the fact that AD obtained 75 per cent. of the vote and over 80 per cent. of the Congressional seats in the 1947 elections, it had to contend with a mounting political opposition. Part of the trouble was that AD was too strong, and as a consequence tended to become too dominant, too uncompromising. The chief opposition came from COPEI. In 1946 the party leader, Rafael Caldera, resigned from his cabinet post in protest against alleged violence done to his party. As the Government tended to become an exclusive AD preserve, COPEI began to absorb landowner and Church elements, thus becoming increasingly rightist in character and increasingly antagonistic towards the régime. On the left the Communists were Betancourt's chief problem. His refusal to co-operate with them or to allow them any role in his Government earned him unbending hatred and the epithet 'Trotskyite'. Inside the labour movement AD forced the expulsion of Communists from most positions of leadership and influence. With URD AD's problems were primarily personal rather than ideological. Late in 1946, for example, the party leader Jovito Villalba was arrested, allegedly for trying to provoke a military coup.

And yet, despite the increasing opposition as its radical reform measures were executed, AD might well have carried its revolutionary programme through to completion had it been able to overcome the one fundamental weakness in its political position—its continued dependence upon the young army officers who had originally put the party in power. From the very beginning AD stuck to an exclusively civilian political thesis. It believed that the armed forces should be non-political, that their function should be a professional and technical one only, and that they ought to be completely subordinate to the civilian executive power. AD accordingly endeavoured to convert the military to this viewpoint. It emphasized that the role and function of the armed forces would always be important and honourable, that AD would always be reasonably responsive to the institutional needs of the armed forces. Fully realizing from the very beginning that their tenure depended upon the goodwill of the young officers of the UPM, the AD junta promptly cashiered all officers above the rank of major, granted salary increases of 30 per cent. to the officers, and increased the pay of the soldiers. In addition, AD sponsored improved living, training, and equipment facilities for the armed forces.

However, the political habits of the military, the result of over a century of tradition, were not something that could be broken in a few years. Despite AD's repeated assurances to the contrary, the army increasingly suspected that AD meant to destroy its status, to relegate it to an ordinary police force whose only mission would be to support the Government. From the very beginning the AD Government was threatened by military conspiracies, at first sponsored by the *lopecistas* and *medinistas*, then by isolated young officers of the October 1945 revolution. As attempted coups increased in frequency and severity, AD began to stir up anti-militaristic sentiment amongst the populace and even made plans, according to the military, clandestinely to arm and train its civilian supporters. AD also attempted to undermine the unity of the army by persuading officers to defect to their party. As a result, tension between AD and the young army officers steadily mounted.

Then, too, the military could not but be acutely aware of the rising civilian opposition to the Government provoked by AD's political exclusivism and its radical reform measures. Opposition political leaders, realizing the hopelessness of their position so long as AD remained at the helm, made their complaints known to the military. The latter were further egged on by industrialists and landholders horrified at the social upheaval AD seemed to be promoting.

AD's downfall finally occurred on 24 November 1948. In mid-November the young army officers issued an ultimatum to President Gallegos demanding that the military be given several additional cabinet posts, that AD should form a coalition Government that would include substantial COPEI participation, and that Rómulo Betancourt be sent into exile. Gallegos refused. The result was the seizure of power by the army and the exile of Gallegos, Betancourt, and the other AD leaders. A three-man military junta was set up. The army thus decided not only to halt the social revolution, but also to return to its traditional role of dominating the nation's politics.

A DECADE OF MILITARY DICTATORSHIP

At the head of the three-man military junta set up to replace the Gallegos Government was Lt.-Colonel Carlos Delgado Chalbaud. He was born in Caracas at the beginning of the Gómez era, but spent his youth in France, for his father, an army officer, had been suspected of disloyalty and was exiled by Gómez. On the death of Gómez, Carlos, who had studied at a French military academy, returned to Venezuela and was commissioned a captain by López Contreras. During the latter years of the Second World War he became one of the organizers of the conspiratorial UPM and played a leading role in the October 1945 revolution. He was one of two military men on the seven-man AD junta, was the senior officer and Defence Minister under the Governments of both Provisional President Betancourt and President Gallegos. During the 1945–8 period, Delgado Chalbaud attempted unsuccessfully to smother the growing antagonism between his immediate subordinates, a group of young Táchira officers headed by the Chief of Staff, Major Marcos Pérez Jiménez, and Major Luís Felipe Llovera Páez, and the AD party leaders. When the tension reached breaking point in November 1948, Delgado Chalbaud cast his lot with his brother officers and led the coup which deposed the Gallegos Government.

The second man in the military junta was Pérez Jiménez. Born in Táchira in 1914, he graduated (first in his class) from the Maracay Military Academy the year before Gómez died. In 1939 he was sent to pursue advanced studies at the Superior War College in Chorillos, Peru. Returning to Venezuela late in 1943, he soon joined the junior officers' conspiracy and became a leader of the UPM. Though arrested before the October 1945 revolution, when that revolution succeeded, Major Pérez Jiménez, as head of a regionalist clique of junior officers from Táchira, immediately became one of the most powerful men in the armed forces. It was he who worked most energetically for the dissolution of the unnatural marriage between the fundamentally conservative army officer group and the radical AD civilian reformers. When the power struggle between the two was resolved by the November 1948 revolution, Pérez Jiménez was elevated to the post of Defence Minister.

Lt.-Colonel Llovera Páez, the third member of the military junta, was a leading member of the Táchira group and an old friend and associate of Pérez Jiménez.

This triumvirate ruled Venezuela for two years, from November 1948 to November 1950. Their immediate task, of course, was to deal with the AD opposition. All the party leaders were either arrested, exiled, jailed, or forced into hiding. The party itself was outlawed. Most of its reform decrees and laws were nullified. The revolutionary 1947 Constitution was abolished, and the traditionalist 1936 Constitution was restored.

Differences over just what kind of government Venezuela should have soon split the military junta. Delgado Chalbaud had promised elections and desired to hold them promptly, perhaps with himself as a presidential candidate. Though he dissolved AD, he was reluctant to persecute former party adherents. His attitude was one of compromise and moderation. The other two junta members, however, displayed little enthusiasm for an early return to constitutional government. They were decidedly inclined towards the military's customary political monopoly and insisted on dealing harshly with AD.

The crisis was resolved by the assassination, under mysterious circumstances, of Delgado Chalbaud. On 19 November 1950 he was machine-gunned by a soldier of fortune, Rafael Simón Urbina, who was shot on the following day 'while attempting to escape'. Pérez Jiménez then became the strong man. He appointed a civilian puppet, Dr Germán Suárez Flamerich, to serve as provisional President, while he made preparations to become the permanent President himself.

On 19 April 1951 the military junta issued an electoral statute to regulate the selection of delegates for a new Constituent Assembly. The provisions were surprisingly democratic. All parties except AD were allowed to participate. There was to be direct election, just as under the 1947 Constitution, and voting was made compulsory.

The military junta then formed a pro-Government party, the Independent Electoral Front (FEI), which was opposed by COPEI and the URD. The régime, apparently confident that it would have little trouble in defeating these two parties which had made such an unimpressive showing in the 1947 presidential elections, allowed Rafael Caldera and Jovito Villalba great freedom to campaign and even publicly to attack the régime. FEI and COPEI called for middle-of-the-road, moderate reform Government, but the URD even outdid the former AD programme in its demands for drastic reform. Its platform was ultra-nationalistic. It protested against the 'imperialistic penetration' of foreign capital. It condemned COPEI as 'reactionary' and FEI as nothing but a façade for military dictatorship.

The elections were held on 30 November 1952. Early returns indicated a landslide victory for URD, for it was leading the FEI by more than two to one with COPEI running a poor third. On the afternoon of 1 December Pérez Jiménez ordered a tight censorship of all election news. On the night of 2 December he proclaimed an FEI victory. He also announced that the armed forces had dissolved the junta and designated himself as Provisional President. Llovera Páez and Súarez Flamerich were sent 'on vacation' abroad.

On 9 January 1953 the FEI-controlled Constituent Assembly met; the URD and COPEI delegates absented themselves in protest. In March 1953 a new Constitution was promulgated, one which—to no one's surprise—granted the President overwhelming authority to rule as he pleased. In April a pro-Government slate of candidates was elected to make up the new Congress, which body, on 16 April 1953, dutifully named Pérez Jiménez constitutional President for a five-year term.

The military dictatorship thus 'legalized', the next step was to make it 100 per cent. effective. The National Security Chief Pedro Estrada built up a huge spy and police organization to achieve this end. Not only were AD sympathizers hunted down, but the political persecution was expanded to include URD, COPEI, and the Communists as well. Jovito Villalba was forced into exile and his party organization was crushed. Rafael Caldera was arrested and jailed, and the Communist Party was outlawed.

True, political liberties had begun to be curtailed immediately following the November 1948 revolution, but with the advent of Pérez Jiménez the persecution became far more brutal and all-pervasive. Thousands were jailed for political crimes. During 1951 and 1952 over 4,000 AD partisans were sent to the notorious Guasina Island concentration camp in the Orinoco jungle region. Here hundreds lost their lives through torture, overwork, malnutrition, and disease.[21] After the 1952 electoral farce, AD sympathizers were joined in prisons throughout the nation by URD and COPEI partisans.

Political parties were not the only ones to incur the wrath and to bear the brunt of the repressive blows of the strong man. The military junta's general policy was to get the workers out of politics in general, and, in particular, to end

[21] Betancourt, pp. 490–500.

AD's influence in the union movement. In February 1949 the Venezuelan Confederation of Labour and all its federation affiliates were dissolved by government decree. Thereafter steady persecution of the local bodies occurred. Hundreds of labour leaders were jailed, and within two years steady police harassment reduced the number of syndicates from over 1,000 to less than 400. Once the AD-affiliated local bodies had been curbed, the Communist unions also came under attack. Then during 1952 Pérez Jiménez attempted to build up FEI-affiliated unions, or more correctly, government unions, but the workers showed little enthusiasm for such paternalism.

Along with its political power labour's power to bargain was lost. For example, when the collective contract in the petroleum industry expired in 1951 Pérez Jiménez, rejecting the demands of the non-Government labour leaders for broad new economic advances, decreed a new collective contract almost identical to the old one, the workers being awarded nothing more than a small cost-of-living adjustment.[22] In a similar fashion, Pérez Jiménez's Minister of Labour settled the 1954 and 1957 collective contracts in the oil industry, and for that matter, all major collective contracts. Thus under the dictator, neither Venezuelan nor foreign employers needed to make any more costly adjustments on behalf of labour such as had occurred under AD.

In the educational sector, the repression was also nationwide. Following the forced disbandment of the Teachers' Federation, hundreds of teachers known to be sympathetic to AD were dismissed, jailed, or exiled. Pérez Jiménez then attempted to launch, with little success, a government-controlled teachers' association. Of course, AD's 1948 education law was abolished, and the protests and demonstrations of the teachers were met with harsh reprisals.

The universities suffered most severely. These traditional citadels of democratic resistance to tyrannical and totalitarian political methods soon ran afoul of Pérez Jiménez.

[22] Lieuwen, *Petroleum*, p. 111.

Student demonstrations against the Government's repression of political parties and labour brought arrests and expulsion of student leaders and professors and the closing of the Central University in Caracas early in 1952. By the mid-1950's hundreds of Venezuelan college students were forced to complete their education abroad, whereas those too poor to do so had to postpone their training. The more 'troublesome' teachers and students joined the political prisoners at Guasina or in the bulging national prisons.

The brief freedom that the Venezuelan press had enjoyed under AD came to an abrupt halt in November 1948. The censorship that began under the military junta was tightened considerably during the presidency of Pérez Jiménez, who imposed heavy fines on mildly critical editors and barred a large number of unsympathetic columnists. Issues of foreign publications in any way critical of the régime were seized. Meanwhile the dictator maintained an official press and fed a steady stream of government propaganda to all the newspapers, requiring them to publish it. The constant vigilance over, and persecution of, the press by the National Security police drove a number of newspapers out of business. The annual protests of the Inter-American Press Association concerning violation of the freedom of the press in Venezuela were simply ignored.

In many ways the similarities between the Pérez Jiménez and the old Gómez régimes were striking. Both rulers were born and raised in Táchira; both possessed inscrutable, taciturn personalities, which depended upon a mixture of cunning, intrigue, and brute force for the achievement and maintenance of their power; both indulged heavily in sensual pleasures and used their high offices for purposes of enormous illicit enrichment.[23]

The parallels between the two in governing philosophy, social attitude, and general economic policy were almost identical. For Pérez Jiménez, like Gómez, had a complete contempt for democratic processes, which he equated with

[23] Tad Szulc, *Twilight of the Tyrants* (New York, 1959), pp. 236–40.

demagoguery. Inept as a speaker and a bungler in attempts to build a political following, he was forced to rely almost exclusively upon the use of force for the maintenance of his power. An inner clique of six *tachirense* colonels, in possession of key cabinet and military posts, were his right-hand men. Immediately beneath them were dependable lesser officers. The loyalty of the officers of the armed forces, he largely secured by high salaries, liberal living allowances, luxurious recreational facilities, and widespread opportunities for graft. Partly as a counter-poise to the military, he built up the National Security police, which was employed to ferret out the disloyal in the armed forces in addition to hunting down the civilian opposition.

Political philosopher and Minister of the Interior under Pérez Jiménez was Laureano Vallenilla Lanz, whose father, with the same name, had held similar positions under Gómez. The old 'Democratic Caesarism' was given a new name, the 'New National Ideal', but the philosophy was the same. The Government declared that the people were not ready to rule themselves. It openly opposed democracy, representative government, and a bill of rights. It repeatedly voiced its determination to '*depolitisar*' (rid of politics) the entire nation and to concentrate exclusively upon material progress, or, as expressed by Pérez Jiménez, 'conquest of the physical environment'.[24]

Material advancement, as defined by the dictator, meant spectacular construction. Many major public works projects initiated by AD, such as the freeway from Caracas to La Guaira, the petrochemical industrial complex near Puerto Cabello, workers' flats in Caracas, the power and steel plant on the Caroní river, and the huge irrigation dam in Guárico were rushed towards completion. In addition, Pérez Jiménez added many projects himself, a number of them of questionable usefulness, such as the Centro Bolívar in Caracas (a semi-replica of Rockefeller Centre in New York City), the most luxurious (and costly) officers' club in

[24] Ibid. pp. 240–50.

the world, and an ostentatious hotel on top of Mount Avila complete with an ice-rink and connected to the city of Caracas by a funicular railway.

Funds to support the building mania came, of course, from the oil industry. Crude production, stimulated by propitious domestic conditions (an enforced political stability and no additional taxes) and increasing foreign demands (stimulated by the Korean War and the Suez crisis) more than doubled production under the Pérez Jiménez régime. Meanwhile government income rose even faster owing to the rise in petroleum prices and the granting of new concessions.

In place of AD's aggressive tactics to increase the nation's share in the profits of the oil industry, Pérez Jiménez adopted a policy of friendly co-operation. By rejecting labour's economic demands and by permitting a one-fourth reduction in the petroleum labour force, he halted the menacing rise in production costs that had occurred under AD. There was no more talk of raising petroleum taxes or of setting up a national oil company and a state refinery. In response to company pressures for new concessions and to his own need for additional funds to finance his extravagant public works programme, Pérez Jiménez abandoned AD's conservation policy. The natural-gas utilization programme was dropped, and during 1956 and 1957 the dictator collected nearly 4,000 million bolivars ($1,300 million) in extraordinary income by selling to the foreign companies concessions nearly as extensive as those they already owned. The justification offered was that such sales were necessary if the nation were to maintain its proven reserves at an adequate level and to prevent the companies from going elsewhere. Similarly the foreign iron-ore producers were encouraged by the Government's anti-labour and lenient tax policies. It was under Pérez Jiménez, during the 1950's, that the iron-ore industry rose to a position of importance in the Venezuelan economy.

With Pérez Jiménez's extraordinary expenditures upon

cement and steel structures, it is hardly surprising that AD's programme for the development of the nation's human resources stagnated. The removal of AD-imposed rent controls contributed to a reduction in the real income of labour despite an increase in money wages that occurred under the Pérez Jiménez régime.

The relative share set aside for education in the national budget was reduced to a mere 5 per cent. of the total (the lowest in Latin America), and as school attendance declined, teaching training was reduced, school construction came to a virtual standstill, and the Government-sponsored campaign to combat illiteracy dwindled to insignificance. Similarly, although Pérez Jiménez completed a number of hospitals initiated by AD, hospital construction fell far behind the nation's requirements, and the AD public health campaign against tropical diseases was reduced.

Naturally, AD's Agrarian Reform Law was never implemented, and its programme to develop the interior by means of irrigation projects, housing developments, agricultural machinery, and farmer immigrants was virtually abandoned.

Instead of AD's balanced development of the whole republic, Pérez Jiménez focused his attention upon making a show-place of Caracas. Over half of all public expenditures were ploughed into the capital city, which under such stimulus trebled in size (to 1,100,000) between 1948 and 1957. The result was an acute housing shortage and expansion of slum areas despite Pérez Jiménez's grandiose flat-building projects. Nearly all the 75,000 immigrants who came into Venezuela during this period settled in Caracas, the bulk of them finding employment in the booming construction industry.

Meanwhile the 'savings' incurred by shelving the development of human resources were diverted to extraordinary military expenditures such as the officers' club, new barracks, jet aircraft, and modern naval vessels, or siphoned off in graft on government construction contracts.[25] Pérez Jiménez is estimated to have accumulated a fortune of over $250 million during his tenure of office, his ordnance chief Colonel Pulido Barreto over $100 million (largely through transportation and parking meter concessions), while lesser officials made away with additional millions.[26] The administration of the Hippodrome in Caracas and the National Lottery, for example, provided vast opportunities of embezzlement for Pérez Jiménez's brother officers.

THE 1958 REVOLUTION

Over the years opposition to the Pérez Jiménez dictatorship intensified. The spectacular public works projects in and around Caracas, though impressive to foreign visitors, were to the overwhelming majority of Venezuelans a poor substitute for political liberty, improved living standards, and honest, responsible government. Even the immense build-up of the armed forces and the police and the incarceration, torture, and exile of tens of thousands of opponents was insufficient to stem the rising tide of resistance to the rampant inflation, the moratorium on party politics, the censorship of the press, the neglect of the nation's health and education, and the widespread official graft, embezzlement, and peculation.

The lower-income groups in the rural areas came to despise the régime for ignoring their problems and concentrating nearly all its attention upon Caracas, while Venezuelans in the capital city resented the obvious favouritism shown non-Venezuelans (both immigrant labour and foreign investors) and the officer group. The urban middle groups in particular—the merchants, industrialists, professional men, and white-collar workers—were deeply con-

[25] See Betancourt, pp. 576–646, for documented details on the economic, social, and administrative irresponsibility of the Pérez Jiménez régime.

[26] These figures are merely rough estimates gleaned from a variety of newspaper and magazine reports. Obviously, statistics on the volume of peculation are unreliable and cannot possibly be well documented. However, the notorious affluence of the exiles and their accumulated assets, both at home and abroad, provide irrefutable evidence of illicit gain on a large scale.

cerned about the absence of freedom and administrative responsibility and the dictator's seemingly reckless alienation of the nation's iron and oil resources.

The university students were in the vanguard of the resistance to the dictatorship. Pérez Jiménez's efforts to crush them by closing the Central University in 1952 only intensified their demonstrations of opposition. Late in 1955 a national University Front was clandestinely set up to overthrow the régime, and from 1956 onwards the student agitation became a growing menace to the Government.

In May 1957 the Church, which had previously remained discreetly silent, came out openly against the Government. Archbishop Rafael Arias first issued a pastoral letter denouncing both the maldistribution and the misuse of the nation's wealth. Subsequent articles in diocesan magazines expressed concern about growing unemployment, vice and corruption, political torture, and the neglect of education. When, early in January 1958, Pérez Jiménez arrested five priests on the charge that they had agitated against him, the Vatican publicly condemned the 'persecution of Catholics' by the régime.

In time, all the political parties became bitter enemies of the régime. Though AD was outlawed from the beginning and thousands of its members exiled and jailed, the party organization continued to function in exile and clandestinely inside Venezuela. *Resistencia*, an AD magazine, was published and distributed fairly regularly, and other publications were issued periodically from exile. AD's secret orders to its sympathizers to vote the URD ticket in the 1952 elections largely explains the surprising URD vote. When National Security agents assassinated one AD party secretary in October 1952, another promptly assumed effective leadership over the underground organization, and when he in turn was captured three months later (and died mysteriously in jail), still another capable leader came to the fore to carry on the fight.

During 1950 the Communists, who for nearly two years

99

had worked out a *modus vivendi* with the military junta, finally went into opposition after their union organizations were crushed and their party outlawed. Early in 1953 the URD, after the nullification of its victory in the December 1952 elections and the subsequent persecution of its party leaders, organized an underground resistance movement. Soon afterwards COPEI, finding it impossible to function under a régime that had virtually outlawed all political activity, was driven into a similar position. All these lesser parties, like AD, issued pamphlets and bulletins condemning the dictatorship.

Pérez Jiménez might have resisted this overwhelming civilian antagonism for some time had he been able to maintain the support of the armed forces. However, control of the army by a tight little clique from Táchira was increasingly resented by the officers of lesser rank, position, and privilege from the other states of the republic. Then, too, the air force and the navy grew ever more restless under a régime run largely by and for the army. Many young navy and air corps officers had received, during and after the Second World War, advanced training in the United States, where they were imbued with democratic ideas and an appreciation of the importance of responsible government to a nation's general well-being.

Pérez Jiménez's overthrow was precipitated by his carrying out of another crude electoral farce designed 'legally' to extend his tenure of office for another five-year term. A year before the expiration date in April 1958 of his first constitutional term, he began making plans to continue in office. In July 1957 elections were scheduled for the end of the year, and URD and COPEI once again began campaigning. The régime, however, fearing another 1952-type embarrassment, clamped down on both parties and arrested several prominent political leaders, including the head of COPEI, Rafael Caldera. In October 1952 the Government announced that it was cancelling the scheduled elections, and instead it would hold a plebiscite, all campaign and party activity being outlawed, under which voters would be given the choice of saying whether or not they wanted Pérez Jiménez to continue as President. On 15 December 1957 the plebiscite was held, and two hours after the polls closed the Government announced that 85 per cent. of the 2,700,000 votes cast were affirmative.

When it had become obvious in the summer of 1957 that Pérez Jiménez was determined to perpetuate himself in office, AD, URD, COPEI, and Communist leaders met and formed a Patriotic Junta, an underground civilian organization dedicated to the overthrow of the dictatorship by whatever means necessary. Arms were smuggled into the country and distributed to the members.

Independently of the Patriotic Junta, as the public pressures against the régime mounted, conspiratorial groups began to form in all three branches of the armed forces. Two weeks after the plebiscite, on New Year's Day 1958, planes from the Maracay air base flew over Caracas and dropped several bombs. This was the signal to the army and navy conspirators that the revolution had begun. However, co-ordination and timing were bad. Army units loyal to Pérez Jiménez marched on Maracay, which capitulated the following day, and several high-ranking army conspirators were either arrested or forced to flee the country.

After this initial attack, the days of the dictator were numbered. To mollify military and civilian antagonism, Pérez Jiménez's uneasy Táchira associates forced him to dismiss both the National Security Chief, Pedro Estrada, and the Minister of the Interior, Vallenilla Lanz. Such moves, however, gave the opposition new courage. Venezuelan citizens, led by the university students, began to demonstrate in Caracas, frequently clashing with the armed forces and the police. The arrest of the five priests already described intensified the popular clamour against the régime. To pacify the navy Pérez Jiménez was obliged to appoint Rear-Admiral Wolfgang Larrazábal, an officer unsympathetic to him, as its head.

On 21 January the Patriotic Junta ordered a general strike. Labour walked out and businesses closed down; industry and commerce came to a standstill in the capital. Street fighting intensified as thousands were arrested and hundreds were killed and wounded. Word of the Caracas uprising precipitated revolts in other cities. On 22 January the navy revolted, upon which a group of army officers, fearing for their own safety and wishing to stop the bloodshed, forced Pérez Jiménez to resign. On 23 January he fled, with all the money he could hurriedly assemble, to the Dominican Republic.[27]

On the same day a junta composed of five officers, representing all three branches of the armed forces, attempted to take over the Government, but the Patriotic Junta ordered the rebellion to continue until such time as there was adequate civilian representation on the junta. Promptly the provisional Government was reorganized to include two civilians on the junta and an all-civilian cabinet. Violence then subsided. The casualties were 300 killed, more than 1,000 wounded.

THE LARRAZÁBAL JUNTA, 1958

Admiral Wolfgang Larrazábal, leader of the crucial 21 January naval rebellion, headed the junta. His immediate task was to dismantle the dictatorial structure. The army, the National Security forces, the police, and the executive branch of Government were purged of known Pérez Jiménez supporters, and Congress, the state legislatures, and the municipal councils were dissolved. Censorship of the press was lifted, political prisoners were freed, exiles were invited to return, and the universities were reopened. Corrupt associates of the dictator had their properties impounded, and many of Pérez Jiménez's military supporters fled the country.

Rehabilitation was the main problem of the junta. Not

---

[27] For a detailed eyewitness account of the January 1958 revolution see José Umaña Bernal, *Testimonios de la revolución en Venezuela* (1958).

only was there the immediate job of repairing the damage of the new revolution, but the long-neglected food, housing, employment, education, and health needs of the people demanded prompt attention. However, the financial irresponsibility of the deposed régime left the junta not only a nearly empty treasury but pressing international obligations to the value of over $500 million. The junta stopped work on the dictator's more frivolous public works projects, but diverted far more than the savings on these into public welfare projects and national rehabilitation and reconstruction works.

As the deficit began to increase, the hard-pressed junta obtained a measure of financial relief at the expense of foreign investors. On 20 December 1958 it decreed a sharp increase in income taxes. The effect upon the larger foreign corporations was to replace the old '50–50' tax law by one which effectively raised the Government's share to 60 per cent. of the petroleum and iron industries' profits.

The junta, of course, was meant to be a provisional governing body only, and Larrazábal announced that as soon as possible he would arrange for free elections and transfer the Government to duly constituted authorities. Within a month after assuming power he appointed a commission of jurists to draw up plans for free, secret, and honest elections. On 23 May 1958 the junta promulgated an electoral law to regulate selection of a President, Congress, state legislature, and municipal councils.

A few days after the January revolution, the exiled leaders of AD, URD, and COPEI had met in New York City and created the Venezuelan Civilian Front, an organization pledged to inter-party co-operation at least until the return of constitutional government. Inasmuch as it was believed that partisan struggles might provoke the military to intervene again, it was decided to nominate a unity candidate for President and to form a coalition administration in which all three major parties would be represented. However, as elections approached, it became increasingly apparent that the political parties were not going to be able to agree on a single candidate. The result was that each nominated its own. All three parties, however, pledged post-election support to the successful candidate.

AD energetically rebuilt its national organization, re-affirmed the reform programmes for which it had stood in the 1945–8 era, and then nominated party chieftain Rómulo Betancourt for the presidency.

URD, realizing the necessity for a strong and popular candidate to defeat AD, nominated Larrázabal. It also adopted a reform platform so radical and nationalistic that it even appealed to the Communists. And Larrázabal not only accepted nomination by URD but willingly accepted the support of the Communists too. This gesture turned COPEI and the church unalterably against his candidacy, and COPEI nominated its founder and leader, Rafael Caldera, who conducted a middle-of-the-road type campaign.

The results of the 7 December 1958 elections were:

For President:		*Per cent.*
Rómulo Betancourt	1,284,092	49
Wolfgang Larrazábal	903,479	35
Rafael Caldera	423,262	16

For Congress:		
Party	*Senate*	*Chamber of Deputies*
AD	32	73
URD	11	33
COPEI	6	20
Communists	2	7

Source: New York Times, 21 Dec. 1958.

Thus AD clearly demonstrated that its national organization had been able to survive nearly a decade of persecution and to retain the loyalties of the Venezuelan people. Caracas mobs, which supported the popular revolutionary hero Larrazábal rather than Rómulo Betancourt, who was well known for policies of reducing the importance of the capital and concentrating on the development of the interior, rioted, but within forty-eight hours political calm was restored. Larrazábal returned to the naval service and was promptly assigned a diplomatic post in Chile, Caldera took his seat as a deputy in Congress, and Rómulo Betancourt prepared, once again, to take over the reins of government.

Chapter IV

THE ECONOMY

VENEZUELA over the past quarter century has had one of the most dynamic economies in the world. Since 1935 an economy that was rural and agricultural has been transformed into one that is predominantly urban and industrial. The change has been accompanied by an ever-increasing national prosperity. In real terms the gross national product more than quadrupled between 1935 and 1960 (from $1,500 million to over $6,000 million at 1953 constant prices). During the same period the population doubled, so that per capita income also doubled.

The chief catalyst in the nation's rapid economic change and development has been oil. Production increased from 148 million barrels in 1935 to 1,168 million barrels in 1962. Petroleum royalties and taxes accruing to the Government began to be ploughed back into the domestic economy, and rising oil company expenditures further stimulated local commerce and industry. Since the Second World War Venezuela's boom attracted substantial new foreign investment, particularly in iron mining, and a flood of European immigrants.

Though the transformation of the Venezuelan economy has been substantial, the process is far from complete. The development of domestic industry is still in the embryonic stage. Many years must elapse before a satisfactory communications network is constructed. The modernization of agriculture is only beginning. Despite some diversification, an exaggerated dependence upon oil still prevails. Though the current trends are clear, the end of the process of economic change and development is nowhere in sight. Whether Venezuela in the future will be able to build a modern,

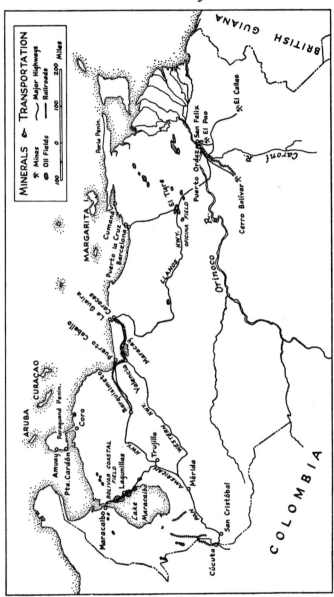

viable, and more self-sufficient economy is still an open question.

PETROLEUM

Petroleum is the axis of Venezuela's economy. It buoys up Government, industry, and commerce. Although the petroleum industry employs under 3 per cent. of the labour force (about 43,000), it accounts for one-third of the gross national product. Oil taxes provide the Government with 60 per cent. of its revenues. In addition, the petroleum industry contributes an equal amount to Venezuelan labour, industry, and commerce as a result of domestic expenditures incurred in the conduct of its operations. Oil company purchases of bolivars to pay taxes and to purchase domestic goods and services provide over 95 per cent. of the country's foreign-exchange requirements.

Petroleum thus explains Venezuela's prosperity, her high national income, her financial solvency, her large volume of foreign trade. Revenues from oil have enabled the Government virtually to eliminate foreign and domestic debts and to invest heavily in development. Petroleum has made Venezuela's currency strong and provided the nation with substantial quantities of foreign exchange, thus enabling her to import large volumes of foodstuffs, machinery, and manufactures.

Petroleum has also made the Venezuelan economy lopsided, dangerously dependent upon foreign markets, extremely sensitive to events abroad. Moreover, the industry's demands for limited domestic goods and services have tended to raise domestic prices, and its payments to the Government, which have had the result of greatly increasing the state's demands, have also helped to raise prices. Thus dollars have become cheap and bolivars dear, so that it is cheap to import and expensive to export. As a result Venezuelan industry and agriculture cannot compete with foreign suppliers in the domestic market without substantial tariff protection, which also raises consumer price-levels, and cannot compete in foreign markets without government subsidies.

There is also maldistribution of the benefits from oil. According to a respected economic analyst:

the chief characteristic of the economy is the high price level for all articles of consumption . . . the costs of which constitute a heavy drain on the limited purchasing power of the population. . . . Commercial profits are large and concentrated in relatively few hands with the resulting savings, lacking normal investment outlets, going in large degree into the purchase of real estate and stimulating a market rise in land values. Thus the great wealth created by the mass production of oil, while largely remaining in the country, becomes overly channelled into inflationary effects, which have no economic utility, to the detriment of its wider diffusion into raising the living standards of the many.[1]

Moreover, the extent to which government revenues from oil have been utilized to promote the economic welfare of the people leaves much to be desired.

As already related in Chapter II, although real commercial development did not begin until after the First World War, Venezuela by 1928 became the world's leading petroleum exporter and was second only to the United States in world production. The great depression slowed down expansion only briefly, and the Second World War gave a great additional stimulus to increased production. Rapid expansion of the industry has continued in a relatively uninterrupted fashion into the post-war period to the end of 1963.[2]

Inasmuch as less than 3 per cent. of production is consumed domestically, the growth of the Venezuelan oil industry has been tied closely to increasing world demands. Since the end of the Second World War Venezuela has been supplying about 15 per cent. of world petroleum needs. The

[1] J. E. Pogue, *Oil in Venezuela* (1949), pp. 30–31.
[2] See my *Petroleum in Venezuela*.

Venezuela
Venezuelan Oil Production, 1921–62

(million barrels)

1921	..	..	1	1942	..	..	148
1922	..	..	2	1943	..	..	178
1923	..	..	4	1944	..	..	257
1924	..	..	9	1945	..	..	323
1925	..	..	20	1946	..	..	388
1926	..	..	37	1947	..	..	435
1927	..	..	63	1948	..	..	490
1928	..	..	106	1949	..	..	482
1929	..	..	137	1950	..	..	542
1930	..	..	137	1951	..	..	622
1931	..	..	117	1952	..	..	660
1932	..	..	117	1953	..	..	644
1933	..	..	118	1954	..	..	691
1934	..	..	136	1955	..	..	787
1935	..	..	148	1956	..	..	899
1936	..	..	155	1957	..	..	1,014
1937	..	..	186	1958	..	..	951
1938	..	..	188	1959	..	..	1,011
1939	..	..	206	1960	..	..	1,042
1940	..	..	186	1961	..	..	1,066
1941	..	..	228	1962	..	..	1,168

Sources: 1921–51, Lieuwen, *Petroleum in Venezuela*; 1952–9, Banco Central, *Memoria, 1959, p.* 28; *Informe, 1962*, p. 224.

strategic importance of this oil is revealed by the 74 per cent. expansion in output that occurred between 1940 and 1945 in obvious response to the extraordinary war demands of the Allies. The Korean War and the crises in Iran in 1951 and at Suez in 1957 also caused additional production spurts.

Eighty per cent. of Venezuela's oil is produced by the world's two largest oil corporations. Standard Oil of New Jersey accounts for 48 per cent. (44 per cent. from its Creole subsidiary and 4 per cent. from its one-quarter ownership in the Mene Grande Oil Company) and the Royal Dutch-Shell for 32 per cent. (28 per cent. from its Compañía Shell de Venezuela subsidiary and 4 per cent. from its one-quarter ownership in the Mene Grande Oil Company). The Gulf Oil Company accounts for 8 per cent. (through its half ownership in Mene Grande), Socony Vacuum for 3 per cent., Standard Oil of California for 3 per cent., and the remaining 6 per cent. is produced by sixteen smaller operators. If production is broken down on the basis of nationality, about two-thirds is accounted for by United States capital.

Seventy per cent. of Venezuela's oil is extracted from the Maracaibo basin, the remainder from scattered fields in the *llanos*. The former area supplies mainly the heavy and medium crudes, the latter the lighter varieties. Of Venezuela's exports of crude and refined products, 41 per cent. is consumed by the United States, 21 per cent. by Latin America, 21 per cent. by Western Europe, 11 per cent. by Canada, and the remaining 6 per cent. by various nations in Africa and Asia.

Before the Second World War, nearly all Venezuela's crude was processed in the Dutch West Indies at Standard's refinery in Aruba and at the Royal Dutch-Shell Curaçao installation. Since 1943, however, the Government has insisted that concessionaires must refine 10–15 per cent. of their crudes in Venezuela. As a result, Venezuela's refining capacity grew from less than 100,000 barrels per day in 1943 to 1,035,000 barrels daily, or one-third of total production, by 1962. The two chief refineries, Shell's at Punta Cardón and Standard's at Amuay, are located on the Paraguaná Peninsula. The recent dredging of a deep-water channel into Lake Maracaibo will probably result in the construction of additional refining plants near the lake shore fields.

Venezuela's proven reserves are estimated at about 18,000 million barrels (6 per cent. of the world's total) or an amount sufficient for about fifteen years' production at the 1962 rate. Until 1950 it had been customary for the producing companies to explore sufficiently to maintain proven reserves at roughly twenty times the annual production rate, but between 1950 and 1956 the discovery of new reserves failed to keep pace with expanding production. To correct this situation, the Government in mid-1956, reversing a policy of ten years' standing, granted new concessions to an amount of 2 million acres. Even so, the total oil concessions (16 million acres) still cover only about one-sixth of

the nation's potential oil-producing area. Clearly, Venezuela is in little danger of exhausting her petroleum supplies in the foreseeable future.

A more immediate threat to the industry is the possible
decline in the demand for Venezuelan oil by her two chief
customers—the United States and Western Europe. In
Western Europe Venezuelan oil is in a poor position to
compete with low-cost Middle East suppliers, while in the
United States the independent oil producers are constantly
increasing pressures on their Government to impose import
restrictions. Also, even if world demand continues to expand as anticipated, the long-range prospects for marketing
Venezuelan oil are uncertain. The possible decline in the
percentage of exports to Western Europe and to the United
States might not be compensated for by the absorption of
increasing quantities of Venezuelan oil by the other Latin
American nations, many of which are developing their own
production.

Venezuela is a medium-cost oil producer, ranking mid-
way between the low-cost Middle East and high-cost
United States. Labour costs are high, the Venezuelan petroleum worker not only receiving far higher wages than other
workers but also benefits in the form of transportation,
housing, schooling, hospitalization, and profit sharing,
which amount to more than double the money wages.
Taxes are also high. The '50–50' formula of 1945, wherein
it was decreed that the profits of the companies could not
exceed the Government revenues from the oil industry, was
revised in 1958 to about '60–40', the higher percentage going to the Government. Added high-cost factors are the refinery requirements, artificially low price-fixing on domestic sales, and the sale of bolivars to the petroleum companies at discriminatory rates. These high-cost factors are offset
by generally low development costs, low transportation
costs (since most of the oil is produced near deep-water
shipping terminals), and by high production rates per well.
In 1956, for example, both the annual production per well

and the gross annual revenue per well were over fifteen times greater in Venezuela than in the United States.[3] The returns on invested capital in Venezuela have been about double those in the United States. However, more relevant in the world market picture is the fact that Venezuelan costs are much higher and her per well production much lower than in the Middle East.

Relations between the Government and the oil companies are closely regulated by law. As previously indicated, until 1935 the companies enjoyed almost complete freedom of action, but since the death of Dictator Gómez the Government has gradually extended its controls and raised taxes. The 1943 petroleum law lays down the basic conditions of company–Government relationships. The various taxes imposed in this law were designed to give the Government a profit share equal to that of the industry, but it took the '50–50' tax decree of 1945 to make this effective.

In the fourteen-year period 1943–56, government revenues from the industry totalled $5,300 million while industry profits over the same period totalled $4,100 million.[4] During 1961, the Government's income from oil amounted to $881 million, while the industry's net profit amounted to $734 million. Net industry investment at the end of 1961 stood at $2,272 million, so that the return on invested capital amounted to 32·3 per cent.[5]

The question of nationalizing the oil industry has not arisen in Venezuela, nor is it likely to. Sufficient domestic capital and technicians to run the industry are lacking. Should the state attempt to run the industry, the foreign technicians would probably leave. Besides, the key to the whole problem is the foreign market, which is controlled by the big producing corporations. Under normal conditions the nation could hardly hope to find buyers; the oil could

[3] Venezuela, Min. de Minas y Hidrocarburos, *Anuario Petróleo y Minero de Venezuela, 1956*, p. 6.
[4] Ibid. p. 159.
[5] Banco Central, *Informe, 1962*, pp. 159, 536.

only be sold in times when world demand exceeded available supplies. Because of the overwhelming importance of the international oil market to Venezuela's domestic economy, expropriation would bring national economic disaster.

IRON

Apart from petroleum, the only other natural resource that promises to play a major role in Venezuela's future economy is iron. The country also produces gold, diamonds, asbestos, coal, and other minerals, but in small quantities only, and none of them contributes more than a fractional percentage to the gross national product. The iron industry, like the petroleum industry, is almost wholly foreign owned and is dominated by two large corporations —United States Steel and Bethlehem Steel.

The iron-ore industry is new. Production in commercial quantities did not begin until after the Second World War. Although the presence of iron-ore deposits in the Guayana highlands region was known to the early Spaniards, interest in exploitation did not begin until the twentieth century. Just before the First World War the Canadian-Venezuelan Ore Company attempted production, but health, labour, and transport problems proved insurmountable.

The Bethlehem Steel Corporation, the real pioneer, entered Venezuela with its subsidiary, the Iron Mines Company of Venezuela, in 1933. It had been attracted by the prior discovery of rich deposits at El Pao, near the junction of the Caroní and Orinoco rivers. Getting the ore from mine to market proved the chief obstacle. Not until 1950 was a suitable transport system developed, consisting of a railway, barges, and ocean-going vessels, so that exploitation could begin.

By this time the world's largest steel corporation, United States Steel, had also entered the Guayana highlands region. Its operating subsidiary was the Orinoco Mining Company. The wartime depletion of high-grade iron ore deposits in the United States had stimulated U.S. Steel to

look abroad. In 1946, while making an aerial survey, it had
the good fortune to discover, west of El Pao, a large mountain of nearly solid iron ore, later christened Cerro Bolívar.
After eight years of exploration and construction work it
began to exploit and export in 1954. By 1960 U.S. Steel
accounted for 85 per cent. of output; Bethlehem Steel for
the rest. A world-market glut led to decline in production
in 1961 and 1962.

Iron-Ore Production

('ooo metric tons)

1950	..	..	199	1956	..	..	11,104
1951	..	..	1,269	1957	..	..	15,295
1952	..	..	1,969	1958	..	..	15,485
1953	..	..	2,296	1959	..	..	17,201
1954	..	..	5,420	1960	..	..	19,490
1955	..	..	8,439	1961	..	..	14,567
				1962	..	..	13,266

Source: Banco Central, *Memoria, 1959*, p. 58, *Informe, 1962*, p. 304.

In world production of iron ore, Venezuela ranked
seventh by 1960, contributing about 5 per cent. of the
world's total. Already, as in the case of oil, she was becoming one of the world's leading exporters, since the other
major producers, unlike Venezuela, processed and consumed most of their own ores. Seventy-eight per cent. of
Venezuela's 1962 iron-ore exports went to the United
States, the rest to England, Germany, Italy, and Japan.

By 1960 proven reserves amounted to 1,000 million tons,
or about sixty years' supply at the 1959 production rate.
Probable reserves were estimated at 4,000 million tons.

Processing the high-grade iron ore (about 65 per cent.
metallic iron) into steel to satisfy some of the needs of the
domestic market has become a government enterprise. At
Puerto Ordaz, at the junction of the Orinoco and Caroní
rivers, a steel mill with an annual estimated capacity of
750,000 tons of finished products was installed; it began
operations in July 1962. Pipelines and structural steel were
to be its principal products.

Compared with petroleum, iron ore as yet plays only a
minor role in Venezuela's economy, but its relative impor-

tance is increasing rapidly. Although its production represents diversification for a country long dominated by petroleum mono-production, it is hardly of an ideal type for a nation seeking greater economic self-sufficiency, for it, like oil, is a foreign-owned, purely extractive industry, subject to the same general price and demand fluctuations of the world market as petroleum.

OTHER MINERALS

Gold mining on a limited scale has been conducted off and on for more than four centuries. The myths of El Dorado and the resulting search for gold was the motive behind the European exploration of Venezuela. Both alluvial and vein gold were found in small quantities during the colonial period, but it was not until the mid-nineteenth century discovery of larger deposits in the Guayana highlands, near the borders of British Guiana, that systematic commercial exploitation began. In 1864 the great mine of El Callao was discovered, and till the end of the century a French company operated successfully here. Peak production was reached in 1885 when 8,439,451 grammes were exploited.

Declining production depressed the industry during the first quarter of the present century, but in 1926 New Goldfields of Venezuela, a British enterprise, enjoyed limited success at El Callao until the end of the Second World War. In 1953 the Government stepped in and helped rejuvenate the nearly defunct industry by sponsoring a state firm, Minas de Oro de El Callao, which has steadily boosted production. Output in 1952 was only 149,000 grams, but this had been raised to 895,000 by 1962. This gold is all consumed by domestic jewellery makers and dentists.

Diamonds are also found in the Guayana highlands region. During the 1930's several companies tried unsuccessfully to exploit commercially. In recent years, however, diamond mining has become strictly a free-lance operation carried out by individual prospectors. Peak production occurred in 1962 with 176,000 carats. In 1961 production was 134,000 carats. Four-fifths of the diamonds are of the industrial variety, and almost the entire production is exported to the United States and Bermuda.

Coal deposits exist in various places along the northern foothills of the Andes. Proven reserves are over 1 million tons, and estimated reserves ten times greater, but for lack of demand only about 30,000 tons is produced annually. Ninety per cent. of this is mined by a government firm in Táchira where the coal provides fuel for the local brick and cement industry. Government plans are afoot to exploit and utilize the coal deposits in the eastern state of Anzoátegui for the developing steel industry.

Production of other minerals includes sufficient salt for local production and very minor quantities of asbestos and manganese.

AGRICULTURE

The agricultural sector of the economy accounts for only 7 per cent. of the national income yet absorbs the energies of 35 per cent. of the economically active population. Thus Venezuelans, in peculiar contrast with other peoples with high per capita incomes, continue to make their living mainly by agriculture. A consequence, of course, of low productivity is low per capita income in the rural economy.

The agricultural problem is an old one. Traditionally the nation has lived by farming and stock-raising. Petroleum did not ruin agriculture, as so many nationalistic writers are fond of asserting. Rather its spectacular development merely made more apparent, by contrast, the backwardness and stagnation of agriculture.

Obstacles to agricultural improvement are both natural and institutional. The country is not particularly well endowed by nature for farm production. The southern half and the northern fifth of the country consist of mountainous terrain which is difficult to cultivate. In the area between, the *llanos*, the annual rainfall is concentrated in a period of a few months, causing severe floods in the wet season but leaving the land too dry for farming most of the year. In the narrow, flat coastal area, the dearth of rainfall all the year round makes for near-desert vegetation. In addition, about one-fifth of the potentially arable land is still covered by dense forests.

Heavy annual flooding has deteriorated, through bleaching, the soils of the *llanos*, and man has assisted nature in the Andean region in making Venezuela one of the most highly eroded countries in Latin America. Years of steep-slope cultivation by migratory subsistence farmers, who burn off the forest cover, and over-grazing by goats has ruined the farming potential of much of the Andean foothill country.

Small wonder that only 2 per cent. of the nation's acreage is under cultivation. The only extensive natural agricultural regions are the Maracaibo and Valencia Lake basins, but even here the concentration of land in a few hands results in much of this scarce good land lying idle. The scarcity of good arable land results in intensive cultivation of small plots in the narrow river valleys and on the mountain slopes in the Andes.

Until quite recently, even the larger farms remained unmechanized, did not use fertilizers, and failed to practice crop rotation. The bulk of agricultural output is probably still accounted for by primitive, unscientific, hand methods.

Ever since the death of Gómez, the state has been concerned by the failure of agriculture to keep pace with the rapid development of the rest of the economy. Yet so vast and basic were the problems of rebuilding Venezuela's agriculture that no more than a beginning could be made before the Second World War. Since then, however, much has been done. Hitherto isolated rural producing areas have been connected with urban centres of consumption. New agricultural zones have been opened up in the northern *llanos*, and European immigrants have been brought in to till them. A series of irrigation projects in the decade following the war—the most famous being the Guárico

The Economy

Dam—extended the area of permanent cultivation by one-fourth. The Government supplies (on credit) machinery, seed, and housing, as well as land. It also encourages production of such specific foodstuffs as coffee, cacao, maize, rice, wheat, peas, milk, and beef, guaranteeing the farmers minimum prices and protecting them from foreign competition by tariffs.

Though food imports rose steadily from $10 million ($3 per capita) in 1938 to $133 million ($20 per capita) in 1956, substantial progress was nevertheless being made towards developing an agricultural base capable of supplying the basic food requirements of the rapidly expanding population. The following table illustrates the success of the Government's programme since 1950:

Venezuelan Agricultural Production, 1950–62

('000 metric tons)

	Refined sugar	Rice	Meat	Fresh fish	Fresh milk
1951	45	15	86	34	36
1952	64	28	87	31	55
1953	71	26	95	32	72
1954	93	31	97	27	89
1955	144	27	101	40	98
1956	198	23	105	39	113
1957	192	27	112		130
1958	157	19	110	59	144
1959	175	39	116	64	167
1960	194	72	121	67	183
1961	215	81	136	65	185
1962	245	103	138	76	187

Source: *Boletín mensual de estadística*, Dec. 1957, pp. 37–39; Banco Central, *Informe, 1962*, Cuadros E3.

By the end of 1960 Venezuela was self-sufficient in fish, maize, rice, beans, peas, bananas, and coffee. Substantial quantities of milk, potatoes, eggs, fruit, and wheat and some meat and sugar are still imported, but substantial progress is being made towards ultimate self-sufficiency in all basic dietary items save wheat. Consequently food imports more and more tend to be of the luxury variety, such as canned goods, cheeses, and liquors.

Maize, or Indian corn, is Venezuela's most important crop. The chief item of diet for the majority of the people, it is used principally for making *arepa* (corn bread) and *chicha* (a type of beer). Nearly all the maize consumed in rural areas is grown by primitive methods by small subsistence farmers, usually on sloping terrain. These *conuqueros* also supply a part of urban maize demands, the remainder being cultivated on large-scale modern farms in the northern *llanos* and the Andean river valleys. Maize production is keeping pace with the demands of the rapidly growing population, but production of a surplus sufficient to feed livestock is hindered by high production costs and the absence of adequate storage facilities.

The high starch content in the diet of the average Venezuelan is further revealed by the production figures which show bananas, yuca, and potatoes as the next most important food crops. These four staples are supplemented by beans, yams, rice, and sugar cane.

Coffee is the chief export crop, as well as an important domestic consumption item. Though grown sporadically since its introduction in the early eighteenth century, it was not emphasized in Venezuelan agriculture till the late nineteenth century. By the eve of the First World War Venezuela was producing over a million bags annually, and was second only to Brazil as a world exporter. Since the rise of the petroleum industry, however, coffee exports have declined over the years by two-thirds and production by one-third. Lower production costs and better soils in Colombia and Central America explain Venezuela's steady loss of external markets. It is only the liberal government subsidies and the growing domestic demands that keep this traditionally important agricultural activity from declining further. Production remained steady at about 50,000 metric tons throughout the 1950's and early 1960's.

Most coffee is still produced on small farms (average 14

acres) in the temperate zone of the west Andean states. Seasonal labourers from Colombia, much cheaper to employ than Venezuelans, harvest a large portion of the crop. The unscientific production methods and low yields per tree characteristic of the family-size holdings is being partially remedied by government financial assistance and technical aid. However, any substantial increase in coffee production will depend upon an expansion of the more efficient and modern large plantations.

Cacao culture has suffered the same vicissitudes as coffee. In the late colonial period it became Venezuela's chief cash crop; then in the late nineteenth century it became second to coffee. After the First World War increasing production costs, disease, and competition from other countries led to a decline. The cacao producers were kept in business only by a liberal government-subsidy programme. Production has since the 1950's remained fairly steady at around 15,000 tons annually, most of which is exported.

Cacao is produced primarily on large plantations along the Caribbean coast. A long-range government renovation programme, aimed at modernizing production techniques and increasing yields, has been under way for several years, but Venezuelan cacao, because of high costs and inferior quality, is unlikely to regain a major position in the world market.

In contrast to the relative stagnation in coffee and cacao, sugar production, under government stimulus, is booming. In the five-year period between 1951 and 1956 production of refined sugar quadrupled (from 45,000 to 192,000 metric tons). Thus the nation that imported more than half its requirements in 1951 became temporarily self-sufficient. Production declined, however, in 1958, and imports were again necessary during 1959 and 1960.

Sugar cane is grown in all twenty states of the republic, but the bulk of it is produced in the warm valleys near the Caribbean coast. The subsistence agriculturists turn the molasses from their low yield crops into brown sugar or rum and consume it locally. The large producers, who also own their own refineries, make the white sugar. Production of the latter has become an important industry. The big plantations and the twelve chief sugar mills that grow and refine sugar employ more labour than does the petroleum industry. The Venezuelan climate and soil are well suited to large-scale sugar production, but high labour costs prevent competition in the world market with low-cost suppliers such as Cuba and Peru.

In addition to food crops, Venezuela also produces some industrial crops. Sufficient cotton to supply all domestic needs can readily be produced in the north coastal states. However, some imports continue because of demands for finer quality cotton. The country's tobacco growers responded to local demands after the Second World War by shifting from production of black tobacco to lighter varieties. As a result, tobacco imports have been sharply reduced and cigarette manufacturing has become an industry of minor importance. Raw material for domestic rope and bag industries is supplied by sisal and henequen growers around Barquisimeto. Sesame is also grown in various parts of the republic.

THE LIVESTOCK INDUSTRY

Ever since colonial times, cattle raising has been an important economic activity. Traditionally this industry has centred in the vast, unfenced stretches of the *llanos*, principally in the states of Apure and Guárico, where the half-wild herds subsist on the tall, wild varieties of grass. In the flood season tens of thousands are drowned or eaten by alligators, and similar numbers succumb to thirst in the dry season. Unpredictable market demands, political vicissitudes, uncontrolled breeding and slaughtering have led to wide fluctuations in the cattle population. There were 12 million in 1858, probably half that number six years later when the Federalist War ended, and only 1·5 million by

1910. Since 1935, although there have roughly been as many cattle as people, periodic meat shortages have occurred, a serious one as recently as 1959.

Since the Second World War the Government has endeavoured to stabilize and improve the industry. It has made loans to the stock-raisers; it has combated ticks, other pests, and disease; it has introduced new breeds of both range and dairy cattle to improve the beef and milk yields; it has provided artificial watering places; it has planted new varieties of grass; it has constructed slaughter houses and refrigerating plants in the *llanos*, thus avoiding the loss in weight incurred by the long, hard drive to the coast; and it has improved meat-transport methods by the use of aircraft and refrigerated truck-trailers. Despite such efforts, a mere beginning has been made on the long-range problem of renovating an antiquated industry.

The raising of dairy cattle has increased in recent years in response to government financial support to local milk producers. Output of pasteurized milk, for example, expanded from 15 million litres in 1948 to 162 million in 1962.[6] There is room for considerable expansion of the dairy industry, however, for substantial quantities of butter, cheese and dried milk are still imported.

The nation has half as many goats as people, most of them concentrated in the north Andean highlands and the adjacent arid coastal zones. These animals provide milk and meat, and their skins are exported. However, such close-grazing animals have been a main cause of erosion, and accordingly the state has attempted to limit goat raising. There are about 1·5 million hogs, mostly in the *llanos*. High feeding costs have tended to restrict the output of pork. Sheep are few in number. Native poultry producers can now meet domestic demands for meat, but not for eggs. The main working animals are horses (used for cattle herding) and donkeys (used as pack animals).

[6] Banco Central, *Informe*, *1962*, p. 366.

FORESTRY AND FISHING

More than half of Venezuela is covered by forests. Diversity of climate and soil produce a wide variety of trees. The most extensive and densely forested area is the Orinoco basin. Here lumbering is presently confined to the triangular region between the Western Andes and the Apure river, an area which includes the three states of Barinas, Portuguesa, and Cojedes. The excellent mahogany stands here have long been the prime object of exploitation. The rapid depletion of the finer woods and the steady advance of farmers into this area will ultimately force the lumberman to shift his attention to the virtually untapped southeastern end of the Orinoco basin. Here, in addition to many different tropical hardwoods, are found several varieties of trees which produce valuable commercial extracts, such as tannin, insecticide bases, rubber and chicle. Similar type forests are also found in the territory of Amazonas at the southernmost extension of the republic.

The Maracaibo basin also contains dense tropical rainforest vegetation in the south with the trees becoming sparser and shorter as one moves northward. In the Andes most of the deciduous forests have long been depleted in the temperate zone, but some evergreen stands are found in the higher elevations.

Lumbering employs only a few thousand workers. Production in 1962 amounted to less than 100 million board feet, three-fifths of it softwood. Expansion of the industry is hindered by inaccessibility and high costs of production. There is only limited potential in the domestic market since wood construction is impractical because of the prevalence of termites and dry rot. The chief value to the country of its forests lies in the control they exercise on drainage and in the prevention of further erosion.[7]

Fishing has traditionally been an important form of

[7] Banco Central, *Informe, 1962*, p. 364; U.S. Dept. of Commerce, *Investment in Venezuela*, pp. 34-36.

economic activity in Venezuela. It was the pearl fisheries that first attracted the Spaniards in the sixteenth century. Today commercial fishing occupies only about 2 per cent. of the labour force (25,000–30,000 men), but subsistence fishing is an important part-time activity for many times that number living near inland rivers and lakes and along the shores of the Caribbean. Venezuelans have always been big fish eaters. Their favourites are fresh mackerel, king-fish, red snapper, salted drum, and millet.

Since the end of the Second World War commercial fish production has more than doubled (from 34,000 tons in 1945 to 95,000 tons in 1962).[8] This has been due primarily to Government assistance in enlarging and modernizing the fishing fleet, and in constructing freezing, drying, salt-ing, and canning facilities. The fishing industry is almost wholly domestically oriented. High costs prevent exports, but improvements in communications, marketing, and pro-cessing facilities could lead to a further expansion of domes-tic sales, particularly of fresh fish.

INDUSTRY

Until the Second World War manufacturing industries were of only marginal importance. The mercantilist poli-cies of the Spanish Crown had built up in Venezuela a colonial-type economic system which prevailed more than a century after the winning of political independence. Under this system export agriculture and extractive in-dustry provided the raw merchandise which Venezuela ex-changed abroad for manufactured goods.

In the colonial era gold, pearls, cacao, sugar, and hides were exported. In the nineteenth century coffee was added to the list; in the twentieth petroleum exports overwhelmed all others. Before independence manufacturing was limited to Indian handicrafts, leathercraft, and crude textile work. Toward the end of the nineteenth century a few small cot-

---

[8] Banco Central, *Informe, 1962*, p. 364.

ton-textile factories were set up, and then under the Gómez régime (1908–35), particularly during and after the First World War, embryonic industries began to take shape. By 1935 Venezuela was making cotton goods, paper, glassware, leather goods, soap, rope, matches, beer, and sweets. Such activity was on a very limited scale, however, and the manufacturers of these products supplied only a fraction of the domestic market.

The Second World War marks the transition of Venezuela from an economy based on agriculture and extractive industry to one in which a third component, manufactures, becomes of equal importance. It was wartime shortages that stimulated the growth of a great variety of new manufacturing enterprises. Employment in factories jumped from less than 5 per cent. of the labour force in 1941 to more than 10 per cent. by 1962. An estimated 281,000 persons (12 per cent. of the labour force) were employed in manufacturing during 1962.[9] Investment in local industry rose from 225 million bolivars in 1950 to 337 million in 1960. Between 1950 and 1962, the manufacturing index (1953 = 100) advanced from 62 to 246.[10]

The following table illustrates the recent expansion in industrial activity.

1962 Manufacturing Index

(*Base Year 1953=100*)

Foodstuffs	233
Beverages	204
Tobacco	280
Textiles	341
Clothing	183
Leather goods	266
Paper products	708
Chemicals	306
Tires	375

Source: Banco Central, *Informe, 1962,* p. 387.

The state has been largely responsible for the rapid growth of domestic manufacturing since the war. Encouragement and support for local industry is part of the official

[9] Banco Central, *Informe, 1962,* p. 381.   [10] Ibid. pp. 387, 396.

'sow the petroleum' policy; it is another important aspect of the campaign to diminish the nation's dependence upon oil. A frankly protectionist policy, characterized by high import duties and rigid import restrictions, has been adopted to shield local industry from foreign manufactures. Also, both local and foreign capital have been further encouraged by tariff concessions on imported industrial raw materials and producers' goods. In addition, the Government often makes liberal loans to local industry.

Despite such official encouragement and the very rapid post-war expansion, there are serious impediments to much greater industrialization. The key problem is the market. The high costs of labour and raw materials, the high local interest rates, and the extraordinary strength of the bolivar all combine to impede development of an export market. Thus market limits are confined within the national boundaries. There may be some room for domestic expansion if per capita income continues to rise, if the quality of local manufactures improves, and if prices are brought down by greater efficiency and lower power and transport costs. At present, however, most Venezuelan industries are artificial inasmuch as foreign manufactures, lower in price and better in quality, would quickly displace locally produced merchandise if import restrictions were withdrawn. Although continued expansion of local industry is rationalized on the ground that this provides large-scale employment for local labour, there is a real danger that too many such uneconomic enterprises will bring increasingly severe hardship to Venezuelan consumers.

The largest segment of the industrial population (about 40 per cent.) is employed in the textile and related industries. At more than two dozen modern mills in the central Caracas–Maracay–Valencia region cotton, wool, silk, rayon, and nylon cloths and yarns are produced. Smaller establishments manufacture wearing apparel sufficient to supply the clothing needs of the vast majority of the population. Similarly, the combined output of several hundred shoe manufacturers (over 2 million pairs annually) is sufficient to take care of almost all local demand.

Food processing has always been an important domestic industrial activity. It has not only increased in response to rapid population growth, but also as a result of the general industrialization drive aimed at reducing all imports, including food products. For example, the rapid recent expansion of sugar-cane output and sugar-refining facilities has in turn given rise to a confectionery industry which now supplies nearly all local needs. So determined has been the national urge to industrialize that even where certain foods have to be imported, such as wheat, domestic processing is encouraged by a high tariff on flour and by subsidies to the local milling industry. The latter, of course, mills the domestic rice and maize crops and manufactures feeds for the cattle and poultry farmers.

Canning is a young, but very vigorous, industry. The opening of a container factory at Maracay in 1953 has stimulated production of a wide variety of canned foods. Several fish canneries operate in the north-east coastal cities, and fruit, vegetables, and meat are canned in the major cities. Only preserved foods of the luxury variety continue to be imported.

The food-processing industry has been expanded to include the domestic manufacture of many products traditionally imported. Thus the meat packers now make bologna sausages, bacon, and smoked hams, the dairy industry has begun to produce cheese and butter as well as milk, and bakery products now include biscuits as well as bread and pastries. Imports of these newer domestically produced food products, though still substantial, are declining.

The beverage industry is dominated by breweries which now supply the country's entire beer demands from imported hops and malt. In addition, soft drinks are produced in the chief cities. Rum making is an important by-product of the local sugar industry.

There is also a wide variety of small domestic industry

which shares the local market with foreign suppliers. These include: the chemical and allied products industries which produce paint, soap, matches, pharmaceuticals, and insecticides; the rubber-products industry which turns out tyres and footwear; the paper and wood-products industries which make containers, household paper products, and furniture; the building-material industry which supplies cement, glass, bricks, roofing tiles, and wood, and the tobacco industry. In such enterprises, in contrast to textiles and food-processing, where the capital is nearly all domestic, foreign capital has participated with local investment.

As a result of Venezuela's extraordinarily rapid post-war modernization programme, construction provides more employment than any form of industrial activity. The main stimulus comes from the Government, with its ever larger road, housing, school, hospital, government building, water-supply, power, and sewage projects. The Bolívar Tower building alone, in the centre of Caracas, cost over $300 million. Further impetus to the building boom has been provided by foreign capital, particularly because of the expansion of the oil industry (including refining) and the development of the iron industry, and by both foreign and domestic capital in the setting up of many new local manufacturing plants. An indirect index of all the construction activity is given by domestic cement production, which expanded more than tenfold in the decade following the Second World War (from 128,000 metric tons in 1945 to 1,450,000 in 1956).[11] In 1962 1,535,000 tons were produced.

POWER AND FUEL

Venezuela's post-war manufacturing and construction boom, as well as her mineral and agricultural development, has taxed the nation's power facilities to the limit. In fact it was an almost chronic shortage of power facilities that kept general economic development from proceeding at an even more rapid rate. Both private companies (foreign and do-

[11] *Pocket Atlas*, p. 62.

mestic) and the Government participated in various projects designed to cope with soaring demands. Their continued efforts resulted in an expansion in electrical power production from only 200 million kwh. at the end of the Second World War to more than 4,000 million kwh. by the end of 1962.

Until quite recently the job of providing electric power was left mainly to private companies. Electricidad de Caracas, a Venezuelan-owned corporation, has long supplied the bulk of the capital's needs. Luz Eléctrica de Venezuela, a subsidiary of the American and Foreign Power Company, supplies Maracaibo and Barquisimeto. Lesser cities have to depend upon inadequate private or municipally-owned firms, and the smaller towns and rural areas are more often than not without power at all. New industry generally sets up plants to meet its own needs. As late as 1950, 40 per cent. of the nation's total installed capacity was owned and operated by the oil industry which supplied its own installations and Venezuelan communities in the vicinity of the oilfields and refineries.

Since the establishment of Venezuelan Development Corporation in 1946, responsibility for providing the nation with adequate power facilities has been increasingly assumed by the federal Government under its comprehensive National Electrification Plan. This long-range power development programme represents a key segment of the overall effort of 'sowing the petroleum'. As such, state power development is designed to support domestic industry and agriculture. Specific objectives of the National Electrification Plan include: the provision of cheaper power facilities to improve living standards and of new power facilities to encourage development of new regions; the renovation of high-cost, inefficient facilities in older regions; and the training of competent technical and administrative personnel.[12]

[12] U.S. Bureau of Foreign Commerce, WTIS Econ. Reports, pt 4: Utilities abroad, *Electric Power in Venezuela* (Washington, 1956), p. 1.

Under the general plan, electric plant has already been built, is under construction, or is on the drawing board for nearly all the cities of the republic. The first important public generating plant, the 30,000 kw. Cabrera station outside Maracay, went into operation in 1949. In 1955 work was inaugurated on a 90,000 kw. unit at Puerto Cabello. The most spectacular development of all was the inauguration in 1958 of the 300,000 kw. hydro-electric station, by far the nation's largest, on the Caroní river. This provides power for the national steel plant there as well as for the near-by cities and towns.

Despite the continued effort, construction of electrical capacity cannot seem to keep pace with demand. Moreover, many years must elapse before such objectives as cheap power and the electrification of rural areas can hope to be realized.

Fuel supplies are almost entirely provided by the foreign-owned oil industry. The companies' local refineries readily supply, at artificially low prices, the various fuels consumed in transportation—principally petrol for cars, trucks, buses, and planes, and diesel fuel for trucks and locomotives.

Industrial fuels and household fuels (for cooking) are more of a problem. Some fuel oil is used, principally by the oil companies themselves, in industry, and paraffin is widely used for home cooking, but the chief demand is for natural gas. At present, except in big cities where pipelines have been installed, natural gas is dear, for it is available only in pressurized cylinders. Work has begun, however, on an all-Venezuelan pipeline network designed ultimately to provide low-cost direct natural gas facilities for home consumption. The eastern and western parts of the country will be supplied from neighbouring fields, which have hitherto burned most of the gas, and the entire centre is to be supplied in the very near future by a line from the eastern fields.

INVESTMENT

There are three general categories of investment in Venezuela: foreign private, public, and domestic private. Foreign private investors are principally responsible for the modernization and development of Venezuela's economy. It was in the last quarter of the nineteenth century that foreign capital, attracted by the liberal economic policies of the Guzmán Blanco régime, began to provide funds for building a communications system (railroads, highways, and port facilities), for opening up mines (gold, copper, asphalt), and for the development of public utilities. Under the Gómez régime, however, nearly all these early investments were liquidated by the Government, largely with royalties derived from the petroleum industry.

Today's foreign investment is highly concentrated in extractive industry, chiefly oil and iron. For example, out of the total of $6,200 million foreign capital invested at the beginning of 1962, 88 per cent. ($5,400 million) was accounted for by the petroleum industry and 4 per cent. ($280 million) by the iron industry. The remaining 8 per cent. was invested in local industry ($180 million), commerce ($200 million), services ($40 million), construction ($30 million), banks ($40 million), and insurance ($20 million).[13] All but 2 per cent. of this foreign investment came from three nations—the United States, Britain, and the Netherlands. The United States alone accounted for 65 per cent., its investors owning more than three-fifths of the petroleum industry, all of the iron-mining enterprises, together with most of the foreign-owned shares in local industry, commerce, banking, utilities, and insurance. Dutch capital (23 per cent. of the total) and English capital (10 per cent.) was almost wholly accounted for by petroleum investment in Royal-Dutch Shell's operating subsidiaries.[14]

The royalties and taxes accruing to the Government from these industries have enabled the state not only to take over from private investors most infrastructural enterprise, such

[13] Banco Central, *Informe, 1962*, p. 147.   [14] Ibid. p. 149.

as transportation, communications, utilities, and power development, but also to enter into business areas previously the exclusive domain of private enterprise.

As a result of the long-range policy of 'sowing the petroleum', the Venezuelan Government has become the largest investor of all. The programme to encourage economic development put the state into the banking business, at first only in a minor way, but its activities soon expanded to the point where the Government became the nation's largest banker. Its huge chain of credit facilities includes the Venezuelan Development Corporation, the Agricultural and Livestock Bank, the Industrial Bank, the Workers' Bank, and four regional Development Banks.

Government-sponsored agricultural development has resulted in the state becoming the nation's largest farming corporation, the chief landholder, the principal food producer, a near monopolist in the fields of storage and credit, all of which were until recently the domains of private enterprise. The Agricultural Bank, for example, which began with a modest programme to encourage agricultural development by extension of credit to farmers and cattle-ranchers, now owns and operates slaughter houses, rice and coffee mills, grain-storage facilities, and cattle ranches, and is the sole wholesale dealer in sugar and rice. [15]

The absorbing tendencies of government lending institutions (principally, the Venezuelan Development Corporation and the Industrial Bank) in the field of domestic industry have been similar. In the building of heavy industry, such as the new steel plant on the Orinoco and the petrochemical industrial complex outside Puerto Cabello, and in power development, it was assumed that the Government would have to play the leading role, but state financing of other enterprise has made the Government the outright owner of, or at least a substantial investor in, textile mills, sugar refineries, pasteurization plants, canneries, and con-

[15] U.S. Bureau of Foreign and Domestic Commerce, *Investment in Venezuela*, p. 12.

struction companies.[16] In addition the state has moved into the hotel business, into mining (gold and diamonds), and during 1960 set up the Venezuela Petroleum Corporation to compete with the foreign corporations in the oil industry.

In transportation and communications pre-emption by the state of all activity by private enterprise is nearing completion. The State Railways Institute now owns all but two small lines. The state is the sole owner of two of the nation's three domestic passenger airlines. The Venezuelan Navigation Company, owned almost entirely by the Government, nearly monopolizes coastal shipping, and is the only regular international steamship line serving Venezuela. In communications the state owns the whole telegraph system and most of the telephone systems, radio stations, and television enterprises.

It has long been the announced intention of the Government to withdraw from any industrial enterprise as soon as development and profit-making reaches the stage where domestic private capital becomes interested in assuming control. The latter, however, has shown little inclination to invest in Government-sponsored business. Its main investment in productive enterprise is in the higher-profit consumer industries, such as food processing, textiles, and clothing manufactures, and the principal investment outlet for domestic private capital continues to be of the traditional, highly speculative non-productive variety (mainly urban real estate).

Joint capital ventures are common. In some government enterprises domestic private capital has a minority interest. Similarly foreign investors hold a minority of the shares in a number of domestic manufacturing concerns.

The most interesting example of partnership between Venezuelan and foreign capital is the Venezuelan Basic Economy Corporation (VBEC), originated by Nelson Rockefeller. VBEC was organized in 1948 to modernize

---

[16] U.S. Bureau of Foreign and Domestic Commerce, *Investment in Venezuela*, p. 11.

food-distribution enterprises. Capital in various VBEC companies has been subscribed by United States investors, by Venezuelan private investors, and by the Venezuelan Development Corporation. VBEC at present operates, with varying degrees of commercial success, several super-markets, a few experimental farms, a fish-processing and marketing enterprise, and two dairy-product firms.

Throughout the present century Venezuela has main-tained an investment climate that has proved attractive to foreign investors. Its key features include little discrimina-tion against foreign business men, free admission of outside capital, absence of exchange controls, almost no nationali-zation or expropriation of private enterprise, relatively low taxes, and a generally friendly and co-operative official at-titude towards foreign capital. But because of high produc-tion and transport costs and the limited domestic market, foreign capital tends to concentrate its funds in extractive industries.

FOREIGN TRADE

From early colonial times until the end of the First World War foreign commerce made up a relatively small part of the nation's total economic activity. The trade pattern was characterized by the export of a limited volume of agri-cultural products (mainly hides, cacao, and coffee) and the import of manufactures (chiefly textiles and hardware). Western Europe was the principal customer.

The war interrupted this traditional pattern and resulted in a marked diminution of trade with Europe and a com-pensating growth in commerce with the United States. The meteoric growth of the petroleum industry in the immedi-ate post-war period was followed by a rapid rise in both the volume and value of exports. By 1926 oil surpassed coffee to become the nation's principal export, and a few years later it had become many times more important than all other exports combined. The growth of the petroleum industry also altered the import pattern. During the 1920's pro-ducers' goods (used by the oil companies) began to exceed imports of consumer goods, and from 1935 on this trend was further accelerated by the domestic industrialization drive. The volume of imports, of course, rose in conjunction with the increase in oil exports, so that foreign trade played an increasingly important part in overall economic activity.

A remarkably steady rise in the value and volume of exports and imports has characterized Venezuela's foreign trade between the end of the First World War and 1957. The following table illustrates the pattern since the Second World War.

Foreign Trade

(million bolivars)

Year	Exports	Imports	Total	Per cent. annual increase
1946	1,625	986	2,611	36
1947	2,168	1,865	4,033	55
1948	3,484	2,752	6,236	55
1949	3,360	2,398	5,758	−8
1950	3,892	2,000	5,892	2
1951	4,534	2,320	6,854	17
1952	4,858	2,545	7,403	8
1953	4,842	2,749	7,591	3
1954	5,661	3,070	8,731	15
1955	6,409	2,959	9,368	7
1956	7,114	3,438	10,552	11
1957	7,928	5,587	13,515	28
1958	7,771	4,783	12,554	−7
1959	7,896	4,720	12,616	0
1960	7,684	3,552	11,236	−11
1961	7,422	3,522	10,944	−3
1962	7,647	3,905	11,552	7

Source: Banco Central, *Informe, 1962,* pp. 97–99.

The value of foreign trade in the period 1946 to 1962 increased at an average annual rate of about 20 per cent. and nearly fivefold for the entire period. As to volume, total imports rose from 1,000 million tons in 1946 to 2,268 million tons in 1962, while during this same period the volume of petroleum exports (which represented more than 90 per cent. of the total) increased threefold (from 388 million barrels in 1946 to 1,102 million barrels in 1962).[17]

[17] Banco Central, *Informe, 1962,* app. tables G i–G iii.

Exports during 1962

	Value *(million bolivars)*	% *of total*
Petroleum	8,057,978	92·7
Iron ore	401,045	4·6
Coffee	62,602	0·7
Cacao	32,367	0·4
Others	134,646	1·6
	8,688,638	100·0

Source: Banco Central, *Informe, 1962*, Cuadro G ii.

As the table above illustrates, four commodities—oil, iron ore, coffee, and cacao—make up 98 per cent. of the value of all Venezuelan exports, and nearly 98 per cent. of the nation's exports are accounted for by the foreign-owned extractive industries.

Petroleum has long been the overwhelming export item. Between 1951 and 1957 the export value of this product increased by two-thirds, or at an annual average of just under 10 per cent. And yet oil's share of total exports steadily declined from 97 per cent. of the total in 1951 to 93 per cent. in 1962. This is almost wholly explained by the rapid growth of iron-ore exports from less than 1 per cent. of the total in 1952 to 5 per cent. in 1962.

Though the annual value and volume of exports of coffee and cacao tend to fluctuate rather widely, there has been no discernible trend towards either increasing or decreasing trade in either product since the Second World War. The annual average for the years 1945–62 was about 30,000 tons of coffee and 15,000 tons of cacao.

The destination of Venezuelan exports is 64 per cent. Western Hemisphere (mainly the United States), 31 per cent. Western Europe, 3 per cent. Asia, 1 per cent. Africa, and 1 per cent. Oceania. The United States alone absorbs over half the petroleum, two-thirds of the cacao, four-fifths of the coffee and all the iron ore. Western Europe and Latin America buy chiefly petroleum products. Since the Second World War there has been a tendency for Western

Europe to absorb a slightly higher percentage of Venezuela's total exports. Over the period 1951–62 the increase was 7 per cent.

Parallel with the soaring volume of exports has come a rapid growth of imports. Between 1949 and 1957, for example, the volume of imports increased by 66 per cent. and the value by 133 per cent. From 1958 onwards, however, imports began to decline.

Imports, 1962

(million bolivars)

	Value	Per cent. of total
Machinery	799	20
Construction materials	223	6
Raw materials	1,224	31
Consumer non-durable goods	376	10
Vehicles	464	12
Food products	300	8
Consumer durable goods	253	6
Other	266	7
	3,905	100

Source: Banco Central, *Informe, 1962*, p. 107.

Venezuelan merchants and manufacturers account for 87 per cent. of total imports, the Government for 5 per cent., the oil industry for 7 per cent, and the iron-ore industry for the remaining 1 per cent. Western Hemisphere countries are the suppliers of 58 per cent., Europe 37, and Asia–Africa–Oceania 5 per cent.[18]

As might be expected, the United States, the chief consumer of Venezuela's exports, is also the overwhelming supplier of imports (52 per cent. of the total in 1962). In 1957 the United States shipped to Venezuela over 1,000 million dollars' worth of merchandise (principally machinery, cars, washing machines, refrigerators, and agricultural products) thus making Venezuela the United States' best cus-

[18] Banco Central, *Informe, 1962*, pp. 107–10.

tomer in Latin America. The United States also supplied
$500 million in services (shipping, banking, engineering,
insurance, profits on U.S. private investment), thus making
the total value of her exports more than $1,500 million an-
nually.[19] Dollars to pay for this tremendous quantity of
goods and services were, of course, obtained from United
States purchases of Venezuelan oil, iron ore, coffee, and
cacao. By 1962, however, Venezuelan imports from the
United States had dropped by nearly 50 per cent.

To stimulate the growth of domestic agriculture and industry, the Government has felt compelled, particularly
since the Second World War, to exercise an increasing
measure of control over foreign trade. Non-competitive
goods and those essential to domestic economic development come in duty free, but high import duties are levied on
items that compete with domestic producers, particularly
food and clothing. Substantial excise taxes are also levied on
imported liquor, cigarettes, and luxury foods. There are no
important export taxes. However, there exists a rather
broad foreign-trade licensing system which applies to both
exports and imports. Export licences are required on any
domestically produced commodities which are in short supply and labelled essential to the domestic economy. Flexible
import licensing requirements on a broad range of domestically produced products (food, textiles, leather, clothing,
cement) are used by the authorities to limit imports to that
proportion of the national market that domestic producers
are unable to supply.

THE BALANCE OF PAYMENTS

Petroleum dollars have generally come into the country
from the growing oil industry at a rate more than sufficient
to compensate for the nation's ever-rising international expenditures. The following table illustrates how until 1958
the surpluses accruing from the international transactions
of the petroleum sector of the economy more than compen-

[19] Econometric Specialists, *Our Soaring Trade with Venezuela* (1957),
pp. 3-7.

sated for the rising deficits incurred by the non-petroleum
sectors, and thus led to a steady accumulation of international reserves until 1957.

(U.S. $ million)

Year	Surplus petroleum sector	Deficit non-petroleum sector	International reserves gold and cash
1953	856	811	457
1954	883	885	455
1955	966	915	496
1956	1,406	1,032	869
1957	1,873	1,378	1,354
1958	1,409	1,800	963
1959	1,490	1,857	596
1960	1,554	1,659	492
1961	1,607	1,626	473
1962	1,554	1,556	471

Sources: Banco Cental, *Informe, 1962*, pp. 132–5, and *Boletín mensual de estadística*, Dec. 1957, p. 100. The extraordinary increase in international reserves during the years 1956 and 1957 is largely accounted for by the sale of new oil concessions.

The overwhelming importance of petroleum in Venezuela's international transactions is further demonstrated
by the fact that the oil industry usually provides over 90 per
cent. of total foreign-exchange requirements. Moreover,
exchange rates are pegged in such a way that the petroleum
sector subsidizes the non-petroleum exporters in the international market, for the oil companies must purchase exchange at below free market rates while Venezuelan exporters receive favourable treatment when buying bolivars
with their dollars.

The introduction of multiple exchange rates occurred by
decree in 1934 after a rapid appreciation of the bolivar and
a corresponding devaluation of the dollar began to cause
severe hardship to Venezuelan agricultural exporters. To
make their products competitive in the world market,
coffee and cacao producers received 3·9 bolivars for their
dollars (the free rate being 3·3) while one-third of the petroleum industry's Venezuelan purchases had to be bought at
the unfavourable rate of 3 bolivars to the dollar. From 1941

all petroleum dollars were assigned a 3·09 rate, while coffee and cacao producers' rates varied between 3·75 and 4·80, depending inversely upon market prices for these two commodities. The fixed rate used by Venezuelan importers remained stable at 3·35 bolivars to the dollar from 1939. The free rate in 1963 was 4·54. The obvious purpose of the multiple-rate system was to encourage development, or perhaps mere survival, of agricultural exports.

These fixed rates for importers, the petroleum industry, and the exporters of cacao and coffee constituted the only element of exchange control in Venezuela. The Government imposed no controls over other international transactions. It placed no limits on the repatriation of foreign capital or profits. It made no restrictions on the purposes for which foreign exchange might be used. In November 1960, due to the growing fiscal crisis, the Betancourt Government permitted the sale of dollars for business transactions only not for speculation or the mere transfer of funds.[20]

PUBLIC FINANCE

Governmental budgeting in Venezuela cannot be done precisely because revenues are highly dependent upon the volume and price of petroleum exports, which are inclined to fluctuate rather widely. Accordingly, the practice has been to draw up a cautious preliminary budget with expenditures assigned to the various ministries on the basis of minimum revenue expectations. Then, over the course of the fiscal year, to the extent that revenues exceed minimum expectations additional appropriations are made to the various ministries. Usually until 1958, when serious budgetary difficulties began to occur, the estimated, or preliminary, budget was about 20 per cent. less than the actual, or final, budget. When deficits occurred borrowing was unnecessary for the treasury traditionally maintained substantial cash balances. Thus the Government was in the enviable position of enjoying great freedom of financial manoeuvre and

[20] For the ending of control and unification of exchange rates in Jan. 1964 see below, p. 185.

could adjust readily to changing situations. Moreover public debt was virtually non-existent.

By use of these flexible budgetary procedures the Government had little difficulty until 1958 in balancing the budget and maintaining a sound fiscal position. The following table illustrates the trend since the Second World War.

Budgets, 1944–5 to 1956–7

(million bolivars)

Fiscal Year	Preliminary budget	Income	Expenditure	Surplus
1944–5	370	614	487	127
1945–6	495	731	754	−23
1946–7	787	1,099	1,065	34
1947–8	1,214	1,562	1,437	125
1948–9	1,610	1,963	1,945	18
1949–50	1,610	1,896	1,928	−32
1950–1	1,632	2,125	2,156	−26
1951–2	1,951	2,297	2,375	−78
1952–3	2,300	2,370	2,377	−7
1953–4	2,362	2,657	2,430	227
1954–5	2,380	2,826	2,797	29
1955–6	2,550	3,200	3,052	148
1956–7	2,670	3,854	3,922	−68

Sources: Pocket Atlas, p. 42; Venezuela Up-to-date, Sept.–Oct. 1958, p. 4.

The above table also illustrates the tremendous growth in the Venezuelan budget in recent times. Adjusting for population increase and inflation, real per capita government revenues and expenditures increased more than fourfold in the period between 1945 and 1957.

The fiscal years 1958, 1959, and 1960, however, were characterized by budgetary difficulties in spite of the fact that over 4,000 million bolivars ($1,333 million) of extraordinary income flowed into the national treasury from the sale of new concessions during 1957 and 1958. During the fiscal year 1959–60, for example, not only was the entire new concession money expended, but the ordinarily substantial treasury reserves were so near exhaustion by the beginning of 1960 that the Government had to borrow $200 million from New York banks and $100 million from the International Monetary Fund to meet expenses.

What had happened to the new concessions sales windfall? Why were rising revenues insufficient to keep pace with rising expenditures? A partial answer to the first question was the treasury drain caused by the unprecedented public works spending spree embarked upon by the Pérez Jiménez régime in its final year in power (1957). As a result, in the fiscal year 1958 expenditure (6,121 million bolivars) exceeded regular revenue (4,411 million bolivars) by 1,710 million bolivars. Virtual completion of the drain upon treasury reserves (still over 2,000 million bolivars on 30 June 1958) was accomplished by the revolutionary junta, which during the fiscal year 1959 incurred expenditures of 7,200 million bolivars while revenues amounted to only 5,000 million, despite the junta's imposition of an additional 20 per cent. levy on petroleum industry profits. Of the 2,200 million deficit, 700 million was caused by obligations of the deposed dictatorship. In addition, the revolutionary junta, electing to sacrifice a balanced budget to popular demands, appropriated 1,500 million bolivars more for the continuance of already well-advanced public works projects, for broad new economic development projects (hydro-electric power, irrigation, petro-chemicals, school construction), and public welfare measures.[21]

When the Betancourt Government took office in February 1959, treasury reserves were near exhaustion, and 2,300 million bolivars in debts were still outstanding from the Pérez Jiménez era. Like the revolutionary junta, however, the Betancourt Government has decided, rather than curtail expenses and arrive at a balanced budget, to engage in deficit financing to the amount of over 1,000 million, or about 20 per cent. in excess of anticipated revenues.

During the fiscal year 1960 anticipated revenues, even though they had been conservatively estimated, did not come up to expectations due to a deepening domestic re-

[21] *Venezuela Up-to-date*, Sept.–Oct. 1958, pp. 4–5 and July–Aug. 1959, p. 5.

cession and a drop in international oil prices. As a result, additional appropriations in the amount of 160 million bolivars had to be made, thus raising the total budget for the year to 6,295 million bolivars. These economic difficulties resulted in curtailment of the budget for the fiscal year 1961 by 13 per cent. to 5,476 million bolivars. However, by the end of the year 1960 it was apparent that the continuing failure of revenues to measure up to expectations would also unbalance the 1960–1 budget, and additional foreign credits had to be obtained to support Venezuela's currency.

Budget for the Fiscal Year 1962

Revenue	Million bolivars	Per cent.
Direct taxes	2,172	35
Indirect taxes	1,803	29
Fiscal domain	1,612	26
Service taxes	152	2
Miscellaneous	164	3
Public loans	334	5
Total	6,234	100

Expenditure	Million bolivars	Per cent.
Interior relations	1,008	16
Foreign affairs	31	1
Treasury	1,493	24
Defence	539	9
Development	150	2
Public works	1,098	18
Education	573	9
Health & social welfare	427	7
Agriculture & livestock	407	6
Labour	47	1
Communications	243	4
Justice	123	2
Mines & hydrocarbons	92	1
Total	6,237	100

Source: Banco Central, *Informe*, pp. 82–83.

As this table illustrates, direct taxes (income-tax) normally account for more than one-third of government revenues. There was no income-tax in Venezuela until the Second World War, but ever since the passage of the Income-Tax Law of 1942 (amended in 1944, 1946, 1948, 1956, and 1958) the percentage of total revenues accounted for by direct taxes has risen steadily. The 1942 law and subsequent amendments were framed with a view to increasing the Government's share in the profits of the petroleum industry. The state's share has accordingly risen from about 20 per cent. before 1942 to 25 per cent. in 1942, 35 per cent. in 1944, 50 per cent. in 1946, and 60 per cent. in 1958. The petroleum industry has always paid the great bulk of all income-tax. Seventy-five per cent. of the total was an average figure in the decade following the Second World War, but the 1958 '60–40' decree has increased the industry's income-tax to about 75 per cent. (about 1,500 million bolivars) of all direct taxes.

Similarly, the 'fiscal domain' item, which accounts for nearly a third of total revenues, is mainly a petroleum company tax. Approximately 99 per cent. (about 1,600 million) of the fiscal domain category income is accounted for by oil royalties. Even this does not tell the whole story of the petroleum industry's tax contribution, for about 10 per cent. (approx. 200 million bolivars) of all indirect taxes is accounted for by customs receipts accruing from the imports and exports of the petroleum industry.

About 55 per cent. (3,400 million bolivars in the fiscal year 1962) of the Government's income is accounted for by taxes on the petroleum industry. Of the remaining 45 per cent., customs receipts, principally from imports, account for 20 per cent., income-tax from the larger Venezuelan businesses and the iron industry 10 per cent., stamp taxes 5 per cent., and various service and miscellaneous taxes 10 per cent.

In the realm of expenditure, emphasis upon 'sowing the petroleum' is evident in the allocation of one-half of the budget to the six developmental ministries (Public Works, Development, Education, Communications, Health and Social Welfare, and Agriculture and Livestock) and the remainder to the other seven ministries whose functions are primarily administrative. The Betancourt Government has encouraged this developmental emphasis, in contrast to the Pérez Jiménez régime, particularly in the Ministries of Education, Health, and Agriculture. The Interior appropriations item includes substantial state subsidies for development.

TRANSPORTATION

The building of a transport system in Venezuela has been closely tied to economic development. Since the dawn of history the natural waterways, principally the Caribbean sea, the Orinoco river, and Lake Maracaibo have been utilized. The only man-made transportation arteries until the late nineteenth century, however, were crude carriage roads between the principal towns and trails for mules and donkeys to haul the cacao, hides, and coffee exports from the places of production to the nearest natural waterway.

In the 1880's, under the Guzmán Blanco administration, British, German, and French investors began building short railway lines in the north-central area which connected the sea ports of La Guaira and Puerto Cabello with the inland cities of Caracas, Barquisimeto, and Valencia.

After the turn of the century road construction began. Government sponsorship of a road network was both politically and economically motivated, for the Gómez dictatorship, in addition to its desire to promote internal commerce, built and used the roads to facilitate the movement of troops to crush local uprisings. At the same time in the petroleum-producing areas the foreign companies began to build all-weather modern roads and to run pipelines down to various shipping terminals.

In recent years the development of communications has

146

become more and more an exclusive government undertaking rather than a private enterprise as in the past. The
gradual nationalization of the railways began in 1936,
when shipping became primarily a state business, and roads
designed to foster industrialization and internal development rather than the extractive industries and agricultural
exports were emphasized. Even in air transport the Government assumed a leading role.

According to 1962 registry figures, the Venezuelan merchant fleet consists of 89 vessels of over 100 tons, with a
combined tonnage of 343,000. Fifteen of the vessels and
63 per cent. of this tonnage are accounted for by oil tankers
owned and operated by the foreign oil companies. Most of
the remaining tonnage is the property of the Compañía
Anónima Venezolana de Navegación (CAVN), a state corporation which is the outcome of the government purchase
over the past generation of various Venezuelan private
companies. The CAVN owns all of the nation's ten ocean-
going passenger-cargo vessels (combined displacement
50,000 tons) and most of the thirty-seven vessels of 100 tons
or more engaged in the coastwise trade and in commerce
on the Orinoco river.[22]

Venezuela's foreign trade, nearly all ocean-borne, is carried mainly in foreign bottoms. Exports are shipped in the
oil tankers and ore boats of the foreign corporations, and the
bulk of the imports come in on United States merchant
ships. The chief ports are La Guaira and Puerto Cabello in
the centre; Puerto Ordáz (iron ore) on the Orinoco, Puerto
la Cruz (*llanos* oil) in the east, and Punto Cardón and
Amuay (Lake Maracaibo oil) in the west. The dredging of a
22-mile canal through the sand bars at the entrance of Lake
Maracaibo in 1953–6 has recently turned the city of Maracaibo into a sea port and the lake itself into an interior sea.

Venezuela's first railway was built in 1877 by British
capital between the Caribbean port of Tucacas and the
copper mines of Aroa just outside Barquisimeto. Other

[22] Banco Central, *Informe, 1962*, Cuadro F ii.

British companies completed the Caracas–La Guaira line in 1883 and a Valencia–Puerto Cabello line in 1888, and a German firm constructed a railway from Valencia to Caracas in 1893. For the next half century there was no railway construction apart from a few short lines in the Andes near the Colombian border and in the Maracaibo basin region between the oilfields and the lake. Between the two world wars the railways lost ground in the transportation system to the developing road network.

After the Second World War, however, an important segment of the Government's long-range 'sowing-the-petroleum' policy was a programme to expand and modernize the decadent railway network for the purpose of stimulating agricultural and industrial development. To this end the Government began to nationalize the private railway lines and to operate them through the National Railways Autonomous Institute. At the time of writing the Institute owned and operated all the nation's railways except two—the Bethlehem Steel line between the El Pao ore deposits and port of San Felix on the Orinoco, and the near-by United States Steel line, which connects Cerro Bolívar with Puerto Ordaz.

During the 1950's the Pérez Jiménez régime planned a comprehensive national railway network. The long-range programme provided for the replacement of the entire 544 miles of existing track, all of which was of varying narrow gauges, with United States standard-gauge lines (1·43 metres). In addition, elaborate plans were drawn up to add more than 2,000 miles·of new lines, which when completed would link all the major urban, industrial, mining, and agricultural centres. Only one small part of this comprehensive programme (a 108-mile standard-gauge line linking Barquisimeto with Puerto Cabello) was completed before the Pérez Jiménez régime collapsed in January 1958.

At present Venezuela has nothing even resembling a national railway network. It has only 650 miles of line, or less than 2 miles of line per 1,000 square miles of territory, and the joining up of the dozen present lines is precluded by the existence of five different gauges. In addition, most routes are badly engineered and the equipment is antiquated. Small wonder that the railways carry only 1 per cent. of the commercial passenger traffic and transport less than 10 per cent. of the freight.[23] At best, the building of a modern railway network will be a long-term undertaking (at least twenty years) and a very costly proposition (probably no less than $2,000 million).

Most passengers and cargo (except oil) are carried by bus and truck in Venezuela. The origins of the present road network go back to the immediate post-First World War era when the Gomez régime constructed the first national trunk road between Caracas and Táchira. Gómez also built various roads connecting the main urban areas of the northern highlands region, and the cities of the latter region with the nearest Caribbean ports. Since 1935 the major engineering defects of the early roads have been remedied; the national roads have been steadily broadened and hard surfaced; oil company roads have been opened to the public (by law); and branch roads have been constructed so that there is a fairly comprehensive, modern, and inter-connected road system.

At present Venezuela has about 20,000 miles of improved roads, about one-half of which are paved. There are three national trunk lines. The most important is the 600-mile Pan American Highway (all paved) running from Caracas through the western Andes to the Colombia border city of Cúcuta. Running parallel to the mountain road at the juxtaposition of the southern foothills of the Andes and the northern reaches of the *llanos* is the lower elevation Western Highway from Valencia to San Cristóbal. The third, and longest, trunk road is the 700-mile Llanos Highway between Caracas and Ciudad Bolívar. There are plans ultimately to extend this road through the Guayana highlands all the way to the Brazilian border.

[23] Banco Central, *Informe, 1962*, Cuadro F iii.

L

An oil-industry road runs along the eastern shores of Lake Maracaibo and joins the Pan American Highway at Valera. Completed during 1962, under government auspices, is a 5½-mile-long four-lane bridge across the neck of Lake Maracaibo, which provides direct land-vehicle transit between the republic's second city, Maracaibo, and the rest of the country. In the eastern *llanos* another important oil-industry road runs northward from the Llanos Highway at El Tigre to Puerto la Cruz on the Caribbean. Over 200,000 private cars and more than 100,000 commercial vehicles use Venezuela's roads.

Petroleum is transported from the producing fields to shipping terminals by pipeline. An elaborate network of feeder lines in both the *llanos* and Bolívar coastal fields runs into big-inch main lines, which, with the aid of pump stations, conduct the oil down to tanker terminals in Lake Maracaibo and the Caribbean.

Difficult terrain, often inadequate roads, and the demand for more rapid movement of passengers and cargo has led to the ever-increasing popularity of air transport in Venezuela. Commercial aviation began in 1929 when a French company began making passenger and mail flights between the capital and Maracaibo, Maracay, and Ciudad Bolívar. In 1933 the Government bought out the French company and formed the Línea Aeropostal Venezolana (LAV), which has since remained the nation's biggest airline. The scope of its operations includes regular calls at all the major towns in the republic. The Línea Aerea Taca de Venezuela, C.A. (TACA), the second domestic airline, is 90 per cent. owned by LAV. These two government lines carry the great bulk of the domestic passengers, nearly all the mail, and a large fraction of the air cargo. Aerovías Venezolanas, S.A. (Avensa) is the only privately owned domestic airline of any significance. About 0·3 per cent of the passengers and 2 per cent. of the cargo transport inside Venezuela in 1962 was by air.[24]

[24] Banco Central, *Informe, 1962*, Cuadro F iii.

Pan American World Airways (United States), which pioneered international travel in Venezuela in 1930, is the biggest foreign airline. LAV, Delta (United States), KLM (Royal Dutch Airlines), Río-Aerovías (Brazil) are also important foreign air carriers. More than 90 per cent. of the international passenger travel to and from Venezuela is by air.

Chapter V

POLITICAL DYNAMICS

BACKGROUND

POLITICS in contemporary Venezuela centres in a power struggle between two major groups of forces. One represents the traditional order—the land barons, the politically inclined military officers, the large merchants, the conservative clergy—all those *élite* elements that dominated the republic from the beginnings of nationhood to the end of the Second World War. They represent the *status quo*. Their outlook is static. They resist change. The other represents the masses of the people—the white-collar workers, organized labour, the landless peasantry—all those popular elements aspiring to a better life. This group is a revolutionary force. It proposes fundamental reform. It demands popular rule, redistribution of wealth, new class alignments. Thus the political struggle between the two involves far-reaching economic and social issues. Venezuela today is in the throes of a painful process of revolutionary transformation. The upheaval is still in the early stages.

The nation was formed in 1830 when the rich landowners encouraged the military to declare independence from Gran Colombia. Though the objectives of the landowners and army officers were dissimilar, they were not in conflict. For the rural aristocracy did not have political aspirations. They merely wished to perpetuate the manorial social and economic system that had characterized the colonial era. So long as their wealth, properties, privileges, and status were preserved, they preferred to eschew political responsibility.

Into the political vacuum created by the disappearance of the Spanish royal authority, then, there quite naturally moved the military element that had led the revolutionary forces to victory over Spain. Politics, to the army leaders, were viewed as opportunities to obtain power, wealth, and social prestige. Though the competing military politicians kept nineteenth-century Venezuelan political processes in turmoil, the feudal character of the social and economic structure was not seriously disturbed. The *caudillos* displayed little inclination toward improving the lot of the poverty-stricken, politically apathetic, and illiterate masses; instead they sought to work within the existing system, using their political offices, as Guzmán Blanco and Gómez did, to amass great fortunes and become a part of the landed *élite* themselves.

For more than a century this military–land baron diarchy held complete political sway. Closely associated with them in the beginning was the Catholic Church hierarchy. As in colonial times, the Church was a wealthy corporate institution with an extremely conservative outlook. Until crushed by Guzmán Blanco's anti-clericalism in the late nineteenth century, the Church co-operated with and supported the landed and military oligarchs to preserve the *status quo*.

Until the October 1945 revolution, political power in Venezuela had been exercised by various regional *caudillos* who successively seized control of the capital. The ruling military clique was generally allied with the landed gentry, for the principal aims of both groups were the maintenance of order and the preservation of the *status quo*.

For a generation before 1945, however, the Venezuelan economy and society had been undergoing a fundamental transformation which rendered political control by the generals and the land barons more and more anachronistic. It was the development of the oil industry in the 1920's that marked the beginning of the end of the traditional order. An economy that was almost exclusively agricultural in 1920 had been transformed by 1945 into one that was both industrial and agricultural.

These drastic economic changes were major causes of—

and also partial effects of—profound social changes. The traditional ruling elements began to be challenged as emerging new social groups—labour and the middle class—started to reshape the Venezuelan environment. The absorbing force of petroleum development and the consequent meteoric growth of cities like Caracas and Maracaibo sucked in labour from the farms and stimulated the rapid growth of middle-class and labour groups. Thus Venezuelan society no longer consisted solely of an *élite* corps of generals and land barons, an insignificant professional and commercial middle class, and a great mass of illiterate rural peons. By the time of the Second World War there had begun to appear industrial entrepreneurs and small capitalists, larger professional groups, and large bodies of literate wage-earners in the cities and the oilfields. It was these new urban- and industry-oriented groups which brought pressures to bear for fundamental political change. As already noted, the chief political vehicle for these new groups was the Acción Democrática Party.

Despite the sweeping economic and social changes and the growth of a large popular opposition party, traditionalist elements were able to resist the mounting popular pressures until 1945. The international crisis produced by the Second World War had helped freeze the Medina régime in power so long as the security of the hemisphere was threatened. But the war also produced pressures that made the maintenance of the *status quo* progressively more difficult. As economic development and social change intensified under the war stimulus, the pressures upon the anachronistic political system became unbearable. Civilian foes of the *status quo* were joined by military ones, young officers restless under a static organization of the armed forces that offered little opportunity for change and advancement. The upshot of this AD–junior officer alliance was the October 1945 revolution, an event which marked the attainment, for the first time, of political power by the Venezuelan people.

Political Dynamics

As related in Chapter III, a power struggle between the traditionalist and the social revolutionary forces has raged ever since. The political dynamics of contemporary Venezuela are perhaps best understood by the analysis of the various components that make up the power complex.

THE LANDOWNERS

The large landowners make up only 2 per cent. of the rural population, yet own 75 per cent. of the nation's arable land. Title to many of their estates dates from the colonial era. So powerful has been this propertied element that throughout Venezuela's entire history it has been impossible to impose any kind of tax on land.

The idea that the landed oligarchy ought to share some of their common holdings with the 350,000 propertyless peasant families was first fostered by a Venezuelan Government in the 1945–8 period. Even though it was proposed that only idle or ill-used lands be distributed and the owners justly compensated, the landed oligarchy bitterly resisted land reform at every turn. It is probably more than a coincidence that the military coup against AD in November 1948 occurred very soon after the passage of an Agrarian Reform Law and before this law could be implemented. It has been a traditional tactic of the landed *élite* to support the opposition to any Government that proposes to tax, or more recently to expropriate, their lands.

A new Agrarian Reform Law, very similar to the 1948 law, went into effect in 1960. The landowners are, in general, determined to resist implementation of the law with every means at their disposal. By themselves they are so small in number that they can exert little effective legal political pressure. Their main hope is again to provoke the armed forces to intervene and oust the present Government. Of all three components of the traditional order, this landholding element is most adamant in its attachment to the old system and in its resistance to change. It has refused to make any accommodation to the new revolutionary forces that are now attempting to remake the Venezuelan economy and society.

THE ARMED FORCES

Though the bulk of the nation's real estate is controlled by a very small minority of the population, an even smaller group, the army officers, which today numbers less than 2,000, has traditionally dominated the nation's politics. 'Venezuela is a barracks', said its founder, General Simón Bolívar, at the time of independence, and it remained a barracks for more than a century later. The history of the nation can almost be told in the lives of its military dictators.

Military rule began with the wars for independence. The soldiers who created the nation insisted on ruling it. The few nineteenth-century attempts of civilians to exert political influence were short-lived, as the army arrogated to itself a governing monopoly. In the eyes of the military, civilian rule was deemed synonymous with political irresponsibility and administrative incompetence.

During the early nineteenth century this military intolerance of civilian political control did not represent selfish praetorianism. The army at first saw its role as that of necessarily having to fill a political vacuum until such time as responsible civilian parties emerged. With the passage of time and the dying off of the revolutionary heroes, however, the patriotism characteristic of early military rulers, such as Bolívar and Páez, began to wane. By the mid-nineteenth century Venezuelan politics were more or less reduced to a battle between competing factions of the armed forces. Particularly in the latter half of the nineteenth century, the caste spirit of the military became firmly embedded, and the armed forces became an essentially predatory institution. Their internecine struggle was little more than a fight for control of the nation's treasury. During the twentieth century, as has already been noted, the military caste insisted on exclusive political control right down to the

October 1945 revolution. Subsequently they merely shared control with AD for three years, then restored their traditional political monopoly in the decade 1948–58.

Since February 1959, for the first time in Venezuela's history, except for the brief periods of less than a year's duration, there has been civilian Government in Venezuela. This in no sense means that civilian forces have come to dominate the military, or that they are at liberty to take actions which might adversely affect the interests of the armed forces. Such tactics led to the overthrow of AD in 1948; the armed forces simply refused to accept either a reduction in status to that of a mere police force or the building up of a civilian militia as a counterpoise to the regular army. Also, they interpreted AD's vigorous efforts to take the army out of politics as little more than a veiled attempt to subvert the army.

Well aware of the military's power to oust it, President Betancourt is treating the armed forces with great caution and respect. He has deliberately over-emphasized the 'important' military role of the 10,000-man army, the 2,500-man navy, and the 5,000-man air force in protecting the nation's boundaries and preserving order. He is not attempting to develop a counterpoise to the overwhelming ultimate political power of the military.

A kind of gentleman's agreement appears to exist. The administration is allowing the armed forces to function as a virtually autonomous official institution. True, the President may call upon the military to preserve internal order, but where institutional military matters are concerned, the civilian authorities have no control. The military's representative in the cabinet, the Minister of Defence, sees to it that the armed forces' customary generous share of the national budget is not revised downward. It is a price the civilian authorities must pay to ensure their own tenure in office.

Of course, there is no guarantee that the military will not again suddenly arrogate to itself the privilege of ruling

Venezuela. That habits a century and a half old cannot be broken overnight was revealed during President Betancourt's first year in office when several conspiracies had to be quelled. It appears that the Venezuelan military are torn in several directions. One group of officers apparently wants to retain the military's traditionally dominant role in politics in order to resist further labour-leftist evolution, or at least slow it down. A second group wants to leave politics to the civilians. Some members of this group are devoted professionals; others, disillusioned over the failure of Pérez Jiménez to resolve major national problems, particularly the social crisis, simply feel that this is a time to stay in the wings. Still a third group actively identifies itself with the reform programme of the Betancourt administration and feels itself guardian of the cause of social and economic revolution.[1]

Which group dominates the military at any given time depends largely upon external pressures operating upon the armed forces. Obviously the traditionalist elements gain strength as political tensions increase, whether owing to landlord resistance to agrarian reform or to a breakdown of the coalition Government. Time, however, appears to be on the side of the professionalist elements and those who believe it essential for the armed forces to make an accommodation with the new order rather than cling to the forces of tradition. If Rómulo Betancourt can use sufficient skill and moderation to carry out his reform programme while at the same time keeping the officers out of the presidential palace until the end of his constitutional term of office, he will have made an unprecedented first important step in helping to rid the nation of the long-standing curse of militarism. Nearly everywhere else in Latin America the day of the military-politician appears to be passing. Several more years of uninterrupted constitutional government in Venezuela will do much to begin to establish a civilian tradition there.

[1] See my *Arms and Politics in Latin America* (New York, 1960), pp. 163–4.

Political Dynamics

Of the three traditionalist groups, the Catholic Church has probably made the greatest accommodation to the recent revolutionary trends. The political role of the Church has varied throughout Venezuela's history. Clerical influence in Government has never been very strong. From the beginning the right of patronage has belonged to the state. Although the Catholic religion was never made the state religion in independent Venezuela, until the middle of the nineteenth century the high clergy were closely associated with the governing conservative oligarchy and in addition played a dominant, nearly exclusive, role in the educational system.

As has been seen, the coming to power of the Liberal Oligarchy in the latter half of the nineteenth century ushered in a period of anti-clericalism. In the 1850's foreign priests were barred, marriage became a civil ceremony, and Protestant religious cults were encouraged. Anti-clericalism reached its most extreme phase under Guzmán Blanco, when the political power of the Catholic Church was all but destroyed. It never fully recovered from the ferocious attacks he made upon its wealth, its position in education, and its spiritual and moral influence over the people.

Though some rapprochement between Church and state began to occur at the turn of the century, Guzmán Blanco's spate of anti-clerical legislation (freedom of worship, civil registry, civil marriage, prohibition of convents and monasteries, prohibition of religious ceremonies outside church buildings) was not removed from the statute books by Venezuela's twentieth-century rulers. Both Castro and Gómez maintained an air of correctness, but coolness, towards the Church, and although, in recognition of its patronage obligations, the state subsidized the Church (mostly in the form of paying clergymen's salaries), it kept the subsidy deliberately low, thus undercutting the strength of the Church and worsening the calibre of the priesthood.

Since 1935 the Church has been making a come-back.

Since Gómez's removal of property-holding restrictions it has become gradually more wealthy and therefore more independent of the state. Though the public education system has absorbed the vast majority of students, parochial schools, supported wholly by tuition fees and Church grants, have remained important and vigorous institutions.

The main reason for the political come-back has been the Church's active intervention in the nation's developing social crisis. Immediately following the Second World War the influence of prominent Catholic laymen was apparent in the founding of the COPEI Party, which evolved into a sort of Christian socialist organization with a strong interest in the welfare of the people. Also, the Church hierarchy itself, by virtue of its criticism of tyranny, administrative irresponsibility, and maldistribution of wealth, played an important role in bringing the Pérez Jiménez dictatorship to an end. This clerical identification with the rising expectations of the Venezuelan masses is in turn strengthening the spiritual and moral influence of the Church.

THE UNIVERSITY STUDENTS

One of the principal catalysts in the Venezuelan political process is the university students. They have been traditionally active in the nation's politics. The autonomous status of the universities has provided the students special licence to participate freely in politics, particularly in revolutionary activities.

In the early nineteenth century student agitation centred in demands for educational reform, particularly in the universities. In the latter half of the century university students became the self-appointed repositories of liberal democratic ideals. They were usually found in the forefront in resisting political repression, in fighting for individual liberties and constitutional rights. In the twentieth century they became imbued with a social conscience at the same time as they began to learn about socialism and Marxism. Dictators might attempt to crush them, as Guzmán Blanco,

Gómez, and Pérez Jiménez did, but they would always rise again. True, student leaders would graduate, settle down, and become increasingly conservative, but there was always a new generation.

It was primarily at the universities, of course, that fledgling civilian politicians received their indoctrination. For example, Rómulo Betancourt, Jovito Villalba, and Gustavo Machado, leaders respectively of the AD, URD, and Communist parties, were all student leaders of the 'generation of 1928' which fought so bitterly against the Gómez tyranny.

Central University in Caracas is the headquarters of student political action. From here are directed several nation-wide student political action groups, each affiliated with one of the various Venezuelan party organizations. The Communists tend to be much stronger in the universities than on the national party level.

The effectiveness of the students in politics is well illustrated by their key role in bringing the Pérez Jiménez dictatorship to an end. Following Pérez Jiménez's 1952 destruction of long-cherished, traditional autonomy of the universities, the students went into uncompromising opposition. They made public protests against tyranny, demonstrated in the streets, and during 1957 worked closely with the underground Patriotic Junta. In the last days of the dictatorship, they led the street mobs.

With the restoration of constitutional government the universities have demanded, and received, restoration of their autonomous status. Student political activity, though again non-violent, is still intense. The faculty is also heavily inclined toward partisan politics.

LABOUR

Of the new political pressure groups that have emerged in Venezuela since the Second World War, organized labour is the largest, most cohesive, and, therefore, the most powerful. Labour probably accounted for more than half of the $2\frac{1}{2}$ million votes cast in the December 1958 elections, and the majority of these votes went to the victorious AD party. The congressional seats won by the Communists were also largely accounted for by the labour vote.

Labour is a new, young force that did not begin to affect the political balance until the early 1940's. It backed the October 1945 revolution, but as a political counterpoise to the armed forces it proved ineffective in the November 1948 revolution. Whether it is at present any better equipped to resist political intervention by the military is doubtful. The effectiveness of labour as an independent pressure group is materially reduced by the close union association with the AD and Communist parties, and by the paternalistic attitude of the Government—though this appears to be declining somewhat—towards the labour movement as a whole.

THE MIDDLE GROUPS

Since the Second World War various middle groups in Venezuela's society have organized, principally along occupational lines, to exert their influence upon the Government and the political parties. The strongest and most influential of such groups are the domestic industrialists (Federación de Cámaras de Industria), the agricultural producers (Asociación de Productores), and the merchants (Asociación de Comercio). The bankers, the engineers, and the lawyers have also combined in associations to form pressure groups. The power of these middle sectors, a heterogeneous conglomeration of unrelated occupational groups, is weakened, however, by a notable lack of common purposes and ideals.

POLITICAL PARTIES

The channels of legal, non-violent action for the above groups are limited to three major political parties—AD, URD, and COPEI. Since all of them are left of centre, favour land reform, and oppose military political intervention, two of the three traditionalist elements (the large landholders and the army officers) can only work outside the existing political system, and, incidentally, outside the law. The Church has been able to work through COPEI. Of the three major parties URD is the most radical and revolutionary, COPEI the most moderate. The ruling AD party is oriented somewhere between the two, though it is by no means a centralist party. It is reform-minded, socialistic, and revolutionary.

Though political parties are becoming institutionalized, the tradition of personalism is still strong in Venezuela. The party leaders still have immense personal power. They are usually able to impose their will and ideas with little difficulty or question. At the time of writing, the leader of the majority AD party is also President of the Republic. As head of the state, his personal, executive powers dwarf those of the legislative and judicial branches of government.

Chapter VI

INTERNATIONAL RELATIONS

VENEZUELA'S relations with other nations have sprung principally from the activities of West European and North American business concerns in her territory. In these commercial ventures the nations most deeply involved since independence have been Great Britain and the United States. Frequently they have been rivals. Generally speaking, Britain's superior sea power and greater capital resources produced for her a position of diplomatic and commercial pre-eminence in Venezuela throughout most of the nineteenth century, while in the twentieth century, particularly after the First World War, the United States attained the predominant position.

BOUNDARY PROBLEMS

Venezuelan Governments, throughout the nation's history, have frequently been occupied with boundary disputes. Once independence had been achieved from Spain in 1821 and once Venezuela had withdrawn from the Gran Colombia federation in 1830, there still remained the task of agreeing with neighbouring powers upon the precise boundaries of the new nation. With the 1845 peace treaty with Spain, the latter recognized Venezuelan sovereignty over all the territories that had formerly been a part of the Captaincy-General of Caracas. However, the limits of these territories were only vaguely defined, and consequently independent Venezuela was saddled with the task of negotiating separate boundary agreements with Brazil in the south, with British Guiana (or more properly, Great Britain) in the east, and with Colombia in the west. Though there were disputes, in all cases these were settled peaceably. However, definite boundaries were drawn in each of the three cases only after prolonged negotiations.

The earliest and easiest boundary settlement was reached with Brazil. In May 1859, following several years of preliminary negotiations, a treaty was signed which provided for a boundary line that was satisfactory to both powers. In the then unexplored south-western extremity of the republic only vague general lines could be drawn, but under protocols signed on 9 December 1905 the last questions concerning the precise boundaries between Brazil and Venezuela were brought to an amicable settlement.

Venezuela's boundary problems with Colombia were somewhat more prolonged and difficult. Under an 1842 treaty, Venezuela and Colombia agreed to arbitrate their disputed border claims. From time to time in the mid-nineteenth century both powers raised the boundary issue, but the extravagant claims of each precluded successful negotiations. After a deadlock of nearly forty years, Venezuela and Colombia finally agreed in 1881 to call in a third party, the King of Spain, to act as arbiter. Both countries based their claims on the principle *uti possidetis juris* of 1810, Venezuela claiming the territory that had comprised the Captaincy-General of Caracas to 1810, while Colombia claimed all of the old Viceroyalty of Santa Fé de Bogotá. The chief difficulty was that the jurisdiction of these two colonial political entities was ill-defined in the south-western part of the Maracaibo basin—specifically in the Río de Oro region. After ten years of intermittent work on the problem, the Spanish monarch handed down in 1891 a decision that the boundary line should be drawn at the source of the Río de Oro river. Since this had never been precisely determined, Venezuela and Colombia were obliged to set up a boundary committee to decide where the Río de Oro began. The committee completed its work in 1901, but the Venezuelan Government not only rejected its findings, but threatened to evict anyone who settled in the disputed area.

Thereupon the Swiss Confederation was invited to send in a team of experts to make a survey and delimit the boundary, but a solution satisfactory to both countries could not be reached. For some thirty years more, until 1932, the findings of the arbitration experts were alternately rejected by one country or the other.

It seemed as though the more that was found out about the isolated Río de Oro region, the more complicated the boundary problem became. For example, when one survey team discovered that the Río de Oro was formed by two other rivers, both disputants promptly laid claim to the territory between the two branch rivers. Not until 1941, after more than a century of intermittent negotiations, were sufficient mutual concessions made so that a boundary line could be drawn which finally delimited the Venezuelan-Colombian border.

Still in dispute was a small group of unoccupied and unimportant islands, the Los Monjes Archipelago, just off the Goajira Peninsula. In November 1952 Colombia recognized Venezuela's claims to sovereignty over these islands, thus terminating the last territorial dispute between the two nations.

The most serious and bitterest of Venezuela's boundary problems occurred in the east with England over the western boundary of the British Guiana colony. The origins of the dispute date back to Venezuela's colonial history. From 1648 until 1814 the area now known as British Guiana belonged to the Netherlands. At that time Spanish possessions practically surrounded the Guiana area, and the Spanish consequently considered the Dutch as interlopers. However, this then useless and unoccupied border region was little desired by either the Netherlands or Spain for neither took the trouble to fix boundaries.

It was not until after Great Britain acquired the colony and after Venezuela became an independent nation that disputes arose. At the root of the question was a conflict of principles concerning the proper basis of territorial claims.

Venezuela followed the principle, inherited from Spain, of basing claims upon discovery, exploration, and royal land grants, and upon this basis, soon after achieving national independence in 1830, claimed as her eastern boundary the Essequibo river. Great Britain, however, sticking to the principle that claims must be based upon the actual settlement of an area, insisted that the border must be located far to the west of the Essequibo. In 1841 the British Government commissioned the German geographer Robert Schomburgk to delineate 'the true boundary'. The resulting Schomburgk line, which sought to establish the western limits of Dutch activity in the 1648–1814 period, extended all the way to the mouth of the Orinoco and included much territory previously claimed by Venezuela.

This jungled 'no man's land' between Venezuela and British Guiana remained the object of alternating claims and counter-claims for the next thirty-five years, but neither party felt it worth occupying until gold was discovered in the disputed region in 1877. Thereupon both countries began pressing their respective claims energetically, Britain extending her claims west of the Schomburgk line into the potential gold area, while the Venezuelans continued to claim more than half of what was clearly British Guiana.

For the next fifteen years the dispute simmered. From 1877 onwards Venezuela made repeated requests to Great Britain to refer the dispute to arbitration, and when these were ignored, she called upon the United States, unsuccessfully, to help her. Finally, in exasperation, Venezuela in 1887 suspended diplomatic relations with Great Britain. For the next eight years unfriendly relations prevailed and border incidents began to occur which threatened peace and served to elevate the dispute to the international plane.

Partly responsible for this was a Venezuelan propaganda agent, one William Scruggs, a former United States Minister to Venezuela, who seems to have convinced the United States Government that Great Britain was the aggressor.

The United States in 1895 declared that Great Britain had violated the Monroe Doctrine and accordingly demanded that she submit the dispute to arbitration. After some hesitation Great Britain agreed to do so. An international arbitration tribunal thereupon resolved the problem. In 1899 it handed down a decision under which settlement was made roughly along the old Schomburgk line, except that Venezuela obtained a small area of gold potential at the southern end of the line and, very important, control of the mouth of the Orinoco river. This verdict settled the boundary issue once and for all at the turn of the century and paved the way for a renewal of diplomatic relations between England and Venezuela.[1]

FOREIGN CLAIMS AND INTERVENTIONS

Venezuela's early national history, unlike that of most other Latin American countries, was relatively free of foreign complications. This was in large part due to orderly rule of the Conservative Oligarchy in the 1830 to 1848 period. They honoured their international obligations, and the enforced domestic stability they maintained afforded protection for foreigners residing and doing business in Venezuela.

The assumption of power by the Liberal Oligarchy in 1848, however, ushered in a period of international trouble of sixty years' duration. Leaders and Governments in the 1848–1908 period tended to be less responsible; they were inclined to borrow heavily abroad, then default on payments. Furthermore, the widespread insurrection characteristic of this era inevitably involved the lives and properties of European and United States nationals, thus giving rise to claims for damages.

The tactics of the foreigners compounded the difficulties. Foreign banking houses often made loans at usurious rates of interest and resident foreigners were inclined to make exaggerated claims for damages. Neither group hesitated to

[1] On 12 November 1963, Venezuela sought to reopen the boundary question before the United Nations, whereupon Great Britain agreed to further discussions.

call on their home Governments to chastise Venezuela if payments on loans or claims were not promptly forthcoming.

Out of the 1848 disturbances came a demand from United States residents to their Government for the dispatch of naval vessels to protect their lives and property. The following year the Venezuelan Government declared a moratorium on payments on loans owed to a London bank, an action which resulted in the British Government's sending war vessels to La Guaira and presenting the Venezuelan Government with a choice of naval bombardment or a prompt agreement to pay debts owed British creditors. That same year Venezuela was forced to sign two claims conventions with the United States. In 1856 a Dutch fleet was sent to the Venezuelan coast to collect damages claimed by its citizens.

The bloody and destructive Federalist War (1858–63) gave rise to innumerable troubles. For example, in 1858 the British and French fleets blockaded La Guaira to force the release by the Venezuelan Government of the deposed dictator Monágas, and in 1860 Spain issued an ultimatum to Venezuela to grant better protection for Spanish property and citizens. During the 1860's both France and Spain sent warships on several occasions to exact claims for damages resulting from the involvement of their nationals in the destructive turmoil and strife that plagued Venezuela in this decade.

The return of stability under the tyranny of Guzmán Blanco (1870–88) did little to alleviate foreign complications, for this dictator was inclined to borrow recklessly in England and France at ruinous discount rates. The inevitable defaults on payments were promptly followed by the appearance of European warships off the coast. In the matter of damage claims, Guzmán Blanco did agree to the formation of mixed claims commissions, which after years of negotiation generally reduced the hitherto exaggerated foreign demands to reasonable amounts and led to amicable settlements, particularly in the case of the United States.

As already indicated in Chapter II, the most serious era of foreign complications and interventions coincided with the rule of the irresponsible Cipriano Castro (1900–8). The 1902 episode[2] had the broadest international ramifications. Germany initiated the crisis in 1900 by laying before the Venezuelan Government a series of claims involving damage to property, recovery of interest on loans, and injuries and losses of life to German nationals. Great Britain soon afterwards presented a similar list of charges. When both were ignored, Britain and Germany, on 7 December 1902, issued a joint ultimatum. Castro's rejection of it resulted in the seizure and sinking of three Venezuelan gunboats. In retaliation, Venezuela seized the crew of an English boat at Puerto Cabello, whereupon German and English warships bombarded the fort and blockaded the whole Venezuelan Caribbean coast. In this latter action they were joined by Italy.

The arousal of world opinion over the growing seriousness of the Venezuelan crisis provoked the United States into offering its good offices to all concerned and resulted in the disputants agreeing to allow the Hague Court to arbitrate for all powers having claims against Venezuela. The claims commissions sat in Caracas during the summer of 1903. The following year the claimants (England, Germany, Italy, the United States, Mexico, France, the Netherlands, Belgium, Norway, Sweden, and Spain) were awarded approximately one-fifth of their original claims. Despite this settlement, Castro's foreign difficulties continued. In 1904 he expropriated the General Asphalt Company for its alleged complicity in a revolt, and this action led to claims for damages and strained relations with the United States Government. In 1906 he severed diplomatic relations with France after the latter charged that her diplomatic representatives had been mistreated, and in 1908 his dismissal of the Netherland Minister brought an assault by the Dutch navy.

[2] See above, p. 44.

VENEZUELA THROUGH TWO WORLD WARS

The assumption of power by Juan Vicente Gómez in 1908 suddenly ushered in a long period of good and friendly relations between Venezuela and the foreign powers. Gómez quickly established financial order and political calm. The numerous foreign claims for damages arising from the Castro era were all paid by 1912. What is more, payments of both principle and interest on the nation's foreign debt were made so promptly and regularly that the whole foreign debt was paid off by 1930. Cordial diplomatic relations were established with the United States and all the Western European powers, and never again did a Venezuelan Government provoke intervention by foreign powers for non-payment of loans or claims.

The advent of the First World War, however, gave rise to a new variety of international problems. The outbreak of hostilities in Western Europe in 1914 sharply curtailed Venezuela's foreign trade and the development of her embryonic petroleum industry. The suddenly reduced national income compelled the Gómez Government to cut back expenditures drastically.

A further problem arose as increasing Allied pressure began to be brought upon Venezuela to declare war on Germany. Public opinion favoured the Allied cause, and there was considerable sympathy in Venezuela for joining the war effort. Gómez, however, long an admirer of Kaiser Wilhelm, was inclined toward the Central Powers. He maintained that there was no good reason to enter the war. He insisted upon neutrality and maintained it. Venezuela, however, was not inclined to forgo the commercial benefits of neutrality, for throughout the war years Allied merchant ships were encouraged to conduct trade in Venezuelan ports.

The immediate post-war period produced a new era of Anglo-American rivalry in Venezuela. This time the struggle was over control of the nation's petroleum. Until the end of the First World War British or British-Dutch companies held nearly all the oil concessions and appeared to be well on the way to monopolizing the entire output. Before 1914 the United States possessed sufficient domestic supplies, but the war's revolutionary effect upon world demand for oil, coupled with Britain's aggressive drive for petroleum reserves, stimulated United States interest in competing with Great Britain in Venezuela and elsewhere in the world.

The competition in Venezuela was extremely intense. By 1920 the agents of several United States companies, assisted by Washington, were seeking leases. Both the British and the Americans competed for favour with the wily Gómez. The latter seemed only interested in encouraging all foreign investors, in the hope that petroleum development and government revenues from oil would increase as rapidly as possible. When United States and British firms hesitated to purchase embezzled concessions from the corrupt dictator, he forced them to do so by threatening to sell them instead to German oil interests.[6]

Till his death in 1935, Gómez maintained most cordial relations with the foreign oil firms and their Governments. The political and financial stability he maintained and the liberal concessions and operating terms he granted were naturally appreciated abroad.

Under Gómez's successors, López Contreras and Medina, the idea steadily developed that the nation was not receiving a fair share of the profits from the foreign-owned industry. As has been related, this movement culminated in the 1943 oil law which revised operating terms in favour of the nation.[4]

Just as in the First World War, Venezuelan public opinion during the Second World War was on the side of the Allies, but again the President was determined that the nation should remain neutral. Venezuela hoped to enjoy the profits without being obliged to take the risks of war by selling all the oil it could to the Allies. Soon after President

[8] See Lieuwen, *Petroleum*, pp. 18–23, 34–35.   [4] See above, pp. 58–59,

Medina assumed power, however, the Japanese, by their attack upon Pearl Harbour, brought the war to the Western Hemisphere, whereupon, Venezuela promptly severed diplomatic relations with the Axis and impounded German and Italian ships in her ports.

During the war Venezuela, to the limited extent that she was capable of doing so, helped patrol the coast against German submarine attacks and defend the petroleum industry against sabotage. Not until early 1945, however, did Venezuela become a belligerent. Her military contribution to the Allied war effort was almost meaningless, but the petroleum she supplied was a strategic asset of considerable value to the Allies.

INTERNATIONAL CO-OPERATION

In the realm of international co-operation, Venezuela has been alternately active and indifferent. On the regional or hemispheric level, it was the great Venezuelan leader Simón Bolívar who fathered the Pan-American movement. At the first meeting in Panama in 1826 (attended by only four nations) Bolívar proposed a co-operative endeavour to preserve the peace of the hemisphere and to protect it against outside aggression. Though the resolutions to this effect signed by the delegates were not ratified by their home Governments, the co-operative-peace and joint-defence concepts ever after remained the principal concerns of the Inter-American movement.

In 1856 the Venezuelan delegates to a Pan-American Conference held at Lima, Peru, took the lead in promoting an inter-American treaty of alliance. However, the Caracas Government refused to ratify the treaty because of fear of foreign entanglement. At an 1865 Pan-American meeting held in Lima in response to the threat of Franco-Spanish aggression, Venezuela proposed (again unsuccessfully) a hemispheric treaty of alliance.

Venezuelan delegates participated in all ten Inter-American conferences held since 1889. However, her contribution to these meetings down to the Second World War was an essentially negative one, for the record shows that she shared with Argentina the dubious distinction of ratifying the least number of treaties and conventions drawn up by the conferences.[5]

Since the Second World War Venezuela's role in regional co-operation has been a more positive one. Her wartime proposals to create an Inter-American Committee on Neutrality, to establish an Inter-American Red Cross Organization, and to define and clarify the status of European possessions in the Western Hemisphere all attest to this. At the Ninth Inter-American Conference held at Bogotá in 1948, it was Rómulo Betancourt who placed the colonial issue squarely before the assembled delegates. He declared that 'the collective faith in the American system had been weakened by the existence of colonies in the hemisphere', and it was obvious that he had Great Britain mainly in mind when he spoke out against the colonial powers.[6]

The Tenth Inter-American Conference was held in Caracas in 1954 in the newly completed University City. The threat of Communism and hemispheric economic problems were the major topics of discussion. Venezuela supported both the United States resolution condemning international Communism and the Latin-American sponsored resolution calling for greater collective efforts to solve economic problems.

Venezuela has also been active in the field of international co-operation. On 3 March 1920 she became a member of the League of Nations. As in the case of other Latin American nations, the record shows that she was concerned mainly with such topics as compulsory arbitration and intellectual co-operation. The Ninth Assembly elected Venezuela a member of the Council in September 1928. However, Venezuela, like many other Latin American

[5] Of the forty-four agreements sent out to the twenty-one members for ratification between 1889 and 1939, Guatemala signed thirty-two while Venezuela and Argentina accepted only five.
[6] *New York Times*, 7 Apr. 1948, p. 9.

nations, became disillusioned with the League during the
1930's, and in July 1938 she withdrew without stating her
reasons for doing so Previous comments by her delegates
indicated, however, that a major reason for Venezuela's
action was her dissatisfaction with the protection given to
small powers. Despite her withdrawal from the League,
Venezuela continued to co-operate with the International
Labour Organization, of which she was an original member, and with the International Court of Justice.

Venezuela's entrance into the Second World War
qualified her as an original member of the United Nations,
and she ratified the Charter on 15 November 1945. She has
been especially active in attempting to establish a more
effective International Court of Justice, one where jurisdiction and competence would be more precisely defined.
Venezuela has also been a leading proponent of the U.N.-
sponsored international Educational, Scientific and Cultural Organization (Unesco).

At the Assembly meetings Venezuela has been interested
in review and amendment of the Charter and has favoured
abolition of the veto in the Security Council. As in the
Organization of American States, Venezuela has lined up
in the United Nations on the side of the anti-colonial
powers. She was a member of the Economic Commission
for Latin America. Her financial contribution to the United
Nations was relatively large in comparison with that of
other Latin American nations.

CONTEMPORARY FOREIGN POLICIES

Largely because Venezuela's geographical and economic orientation is seaward rather than towards continental
South America, she has been deeply involved in the ideological struggle between dictatorship and democracy in the
Caribbean area, particularly since the Second World War.
Her policy has understandably fluctuated with the political
complexion of her Governments. During the 1945–8 period,
when Democratic Action was in power, the nation adopted

an aggressive attitude towards dictatorship everywhere, severing diplomatic relations with the Dominican Republic (and also with Spain) and being decidedly cool in dealing with Nicaragua. However, in 1949 Pérez Jiménez re-established relations with Rafael Trujillo (and also with Francisco Franco) and friendship with Anastasio Somoza of Nicaragua, and he was antagonistic toward the democratic régime of José Figueres in Costa Rica. Following the return of democratic, constitutional government to Venezuela in 1959, hostility towards the dictatorships and friendship towards the democracies of the Caribbean once more characterized Venezuela's foreign policy.

Chapter VII

THE BETANCOURT GOVERNMENT

THE 1961 CONSTITUTION

On 13 February 1959 Rómulo Betancourt was inaugurated constitutional President of Venezuela for a five-year term of office scheduled to end on 4 March 1964. Although the 1953 Constitution was theoretically still in force, the new Government in practice operated for nearly two years under the general principles of the 1947 Constitution. Meanwhile, a new Constitution was drafted by a committee and then debated and revised by Congress. It went into effect on 23 January 1961 the third anniversary of the overthrow of the Pérez Jiménez dictatorship.

The 1961 Constitution, like that of 1947, reflected the political philosophy of the President and the Acción Democrática Party. In sharp contradistinction to the 1953 document, it was concerned with 'protecting and uplifting labor, upholding human dignity, promoting general well-being and social security; achieving an equitable participation by all in the enjoyment of wealth, according to principles of social justice, and promoting the development of the economy in the service of man'. The noble ideals of the preamble were spelled out in various articles. Labour rights included a maximum working week of 48 hours (later reduced to 40) and a fair minimum wage; freedom to organize, to bargain collectively, and to strike; and a system of social security. Article 95 provided for an economic system 'based on principles of social justice' and required the state to 'promote economic development . . . in order to . . . increase the income level of the population'. Although protection for private property was guaranteed (Article 99), the system of latifundia was proclaimed 'contrary to the social interest' (Article 105). Specific social obligations of the Government included protection of the family nucleus, maintenance of public health, improvement of the living conditions of the peasantry, and provision of educational opportunities for all (Articles 73–78).

HUMAN RESOURCE DEVELOPMENT

With the aid of an initially co-operative Congress, the Betancourt Government promptly launched a vigorous programme in all those human-resource areas so badly neglected by Pérez Jiménez. The education budget was more than doubled. An emergency school-construction and teacher-training programme was started in 1959, its aim being to provide educational facilities to the more than half a million school-aged children who lacked them. By the end of 1962, this goal was 97 per cent. achieved. Perhaps an even more ambitious undertaking was the campaign against adult illiteracy, estimated at 57 per cent. when the new Government took office. Twelve thousand literacy centres were set up in an all-out effort to teach everyone to read and write by the time the president's term ended. This goal was only half achieved, as one of every four Venezuelans over the age of ten was still illiterate at the beginning of 1964.

In the field of health, hospital construction, the training of additional doctors and nurses, and intensified war upon tropical diseases were the chief components of the Government's emergency 'human resource' development programme. Again, as in education, the monies poured into the national health programme more than doubled during the years 1959 to 1964. Though hospitals and beds were still insufficient to provide for national needs by 1964, the 1959 health-facility shortage was appreciably reduced. During the early 1960's, smallpox and malaria were virtually eliminated; Chagas disease, typhoid, and tuberculosis were drastically reduced; but dysentery still claimed the lives of 112 of every 100,000 persons annually.

In the general realm of social improvements, the urban

housing problem was one on which very little progress was made. The half-million permanent-dwelling deficit inherited from the Pérez Jiménez dictatorship increased substantially during the years 1959–64. The Government's modest urban-housing programme was hardly sufficient to keep pace with the more than 3 per cent. annual population increase, let alone provide for the continued migration from farm to city. The census of 26 February 1961 revealed a population of 7,555,799 (a 50 per cent. growth since 1950), of which 67·5 per cent. were urban dwellers (as compared with 53·8 per cent. in 1950).[1]

In an effort to halt the rural exodus, priority in government expenditure went to the countryside. As soon as the new administration took office early in 1959 it began giving away public lands to the peasantry, the key supporters of the Acción Democrática Party. This *ad hoc* distribution policy continued for a full year until 5 March 1960, when the Agrarian Reform Law, the fundamental legislative act of the Betancourt Government, was promulgated. Under it, the National Agrarian Institute began granting land titles outright to individuals and in joint ownership to co-operatives. The law provided not only for continued distribution of public lands, but also for breaking up the large estates. Landowners cultivating their properties fully and wisely were exempted from expropriation, but holders of idle lands were persuaded, partly by new taxes, to sell, and if they refused, the law sanctioned outright expropriation. Under either method, government appraisers attempted to arrive at a fair market valuation, upon which the owner was compensated fully in cash, partly in negotiable government bonds.

The President's announced goal was to redistribute enough land during his term of office to provide farms for more than half the estimated 300,000 rural families who were landless at the time of the passage of the Agrarian

---

[1] See Min. de Fomento, *IX Censo de Población* (Caracas, 1962). The population at the beginning of 1964 was estimated at 8·5 million.

Reform Law. This aim was only partially achieved. The number of peasants in need of land was somewhat over-estimated (less than 200,000 applications were received), but 75,000 family heads received about 5 million acres of land between 1959 and 1964.

On the other hand, the obstacles to, and complexities of, agrarian reform had been underestimated. Once the desirable public lands began to give out, the National Agrarian Institute was without adequate funds to purchase private holdings. Also, the building of a rural infrastructure, upon which the prosperity of the agricultural sector of the economy was dependent, was a slow, costly process. In addition to the aforementioned schools and health facilities, the Ministry of Public Works was obliged to begin the development of a comprehensive system of irrigation projects and market-access roads. Furthermore, the manifold problems of rural housing (about 20,000 units were provided), sanitary water supplies, modern farm machinery, technical training, and agricultural credits had to be tackled.

All-in-all, however, an impressive beginning on a most difficult long-range problem was made. Agricultural output not only kept pace with population growth but expanded at a sufficient rate to allow for a modest, though steady, decline in food imports. Despite the difficulties, complaints, and shortcomings of the programme, rural Venezuela demonstrated, on balance, broad support for the Government's programme. It refused to co-operate with sporadic Castro-Communist guerrilla activities, and it provided the Government with the margin of victory in the presidential and congressional elections of 1 December 1963.

Organized labour (rural, urban, industrial, mining, and petroleum) was the principal political prop of the Betancourt administration. During its first year in power most of the 600 unions existing at the time of Pérez Jiménez's downfall were reorganized and more than 700 new unions were legalized.[2] National federations, the most important of which were the construction, transport, petroleum, and farm workers' groups, were re-established, and the Venezuelan Confederation of Labour, representing 1,100,000 employees, was revived. After two years, however, the almost monolithic labour support of the administration began to erode, this erosion being a reflection of two serious splits in the Acción Democrática Party and a partial breakdown of the Government coalition. In fact, by mid-1962, labour was definitely bifurcated into pro- and anti-government branches. The latter set up a rival 'anti-officialist' Central Confederation of Labour, which was much more radical and Marxist-oriented than the original confederation. However, the administration retained the support of the majority of organized labour. This was demonstrated in the repeated failure of general strike calls by anti-government unions and by the election, on 1 December 1963, of Raúl Leoni, the candidate who had won his political spurs as Acción Democrática's actively reforming Labour Minister in 1945–8.

Of course, with the return of a free labour movement, employers in the major industries were obliged to bargain collectively once more with the labour federations. With government backing, long-term collective contracts were signed by the major federations and their employers. Nearly always wage increases, reduction in working hours, and fringe benefits resulted. The most important of the contracts was that between the Federation of Petroleum Workers and the oil industry, signed in February 1960. Under it some 40,000 workers received additional annual benefits estimated at $100 million, the costs of which were divided by the industry and the Government. Three years later, another collective petroleum contract, further increasing the benefits to the workers, was signed.

[2] By 1964 there were nearly 2,000 local branches organized into regional and industrial federations.

MATERIAL RESOURCE DEVELOPMENT

Concurrently with its human resource development programme, in the fields of education, health, agrarian reform, and labour, the Betancourt administration attempted to carry out a carefully planned programme for development of Venezuela's material resources. Of course, the agrarian-reform programme had material as well as human ends, namely self-sufficiency in food production—a goal approached but by no means attained. Another facet of material development was a programme of substantial public investment in communications, including improved and expanded roads, railways, airports, and shipping facilities.

However, the major effort in the material resource development programme was in the field of domestic industry. Industrialization was viewed both as a means for reducing the country's traditional heavy dependence upon manufactured goods and as a panacea for the disturbing problem of unemployment (about 13 per cent. of the labour force in 1959). Despite government stimulus to private enterprise, both foreign and domestic, in the form of concessions, credits, protective tariffs, and special tax advantages, the results were not encouraging. Industrial output rose only 2 per cent. in 1960, 4·6 per cent. in 1961, and 9 per cent. in 1962 (compared with a 14 per cent. average annual increase during the 1950's), and unemployment was not appreciably reduced. Late in 1962, the President made a renewed effort to attract foreign capital into manufacturing by signing with the United States an investment-guarantee programme which provided foreign investors with protection against expropriation and inconvertibility.

The administration tried to compensate for disappointments in the private sector by pushing ahead with government-sponsored enterprises. The largest of these was the Guayana Corporation, created in 1960 to promote integrated development of the rich mineral and hydro-electric power resources of south-eastern Venezuela, where iron mining had begun a decade earlier. In the geographic centre of the region, near the junction of the Orinoco and Caroní rivers, was founded the model city of San Tomé de Guayana. Heart of the growing industrial complex was the Government's Orinoco Steel Plant (inaugurated July 1962) conveniently powered by the huge Caroní hydro-electric station (inaugurated April 1959). Complementing these installations was the new Reynolds Aluminium plant, a joint private enterprise-government venture. The administration encouraged internal migrants and foreign capitalists to help develop the area into 'the Ruhr of South America'. By early 1964 San Tomé had 50,000 people and settlers were arriving at the rate of 1,000 per month.

OIL POLICY

The Government also moved into the hitherto wholly foreign-owned petroleum industry. In April 1961, it created the Venezuelan Petroleum Corporation, a state-owned enterprise set up to exploit national reserve parcels and compete with the foreign corporations in exploration, production, refining, and marketing. Up to 1964, however, these aims remained little more than symbolic aspirations. Lacking capital, the state company was in no position to make the investments required. Also, it had a problem of marketing outlets. Accordingly, it confined itself to minor exploitation contracts with the large foreign operators.

The Government's petroleum policy in general was a continuation of that which was interrupted in 1948. It was made clear that, in line with conservation policies and national aspirations, under no conditions would new concessions be granted. Thus all new development in petroleum was sealed off from private enterprise. Although the companies were assured that their tax burdens would not be increased, the Government tried to increase its petroleum revenues by controlling export prices. Irked by the post–1959 price decline caused by world overproduction, Mines Minister Juan Pablo Pérez Alfonso initiated the formation in 1960 of the Organization of Petroleum Exporting Countries (OPEC). It was first agreed that OPEC should promote price control and the sharing out of production among member countries. Venezuela, however, was in a minority of one against the Middle and Far Eastern countries (Iraq, Iran, Kuwait, Saudi Arabia, later joined by Qatar, Libya, and Indonesia); and by 1963 OPEC was chiefly concerned with securing a larger share of the oil companies' earnings. Venezuela's position *vis-à-vis* the Middle East had deteriorated: her share of the output of OPEC countries had fallen from 39·3 per cent, in 1959 to 35·6 per cent. in 1962, and in 1963 her own output only increased by 2 per cent. as compared with 4 per cent. for the Middle East.[3] Venezuelan crude oil production continued to inch up annually from 1,011 million barrels in 1959 to 1,168 million in 1962, while prices remained somewhat depressed.

ADMINISTRATIVE REFORM

Administrative reform also received considerable attention from the Betancourt Government. War was declared on corruption, still prevalent in the intermediate levels of the bureaucracy, by imposing tighter auditing controls and stiffer penalties for peculation. Also, a civil-service merit system began to be introduced. Expenditures were better regulated by an overhaul of the Comptroller General's office and the framing of an Organic Budget Law, while collections rose substantially following implementation of the February 1961 Tax Reform Law. Measures such as these, plus an austerity programme, enabled the Government to overcome both the fiscal problems inherited from the dictatorship and those resulting from the 1959–61 recession. In fiscal 1963, the

[3] Geoffrey Drayton, 'The Travails of OPEC', *World Today*, Nov. 1963.

President was able, for the first time, to present a balanced budget without serious curtailment of his human and material resource development programmes.

Most of the President's term was spent combating the stubborn economic problem. Following the fall of the dictator and the resulting political instability, there occurred a flight of capital so substantial that a liquidity crisis ensued. This forced the Government to institute modified exchange controls in November 1960. Further to halt the decline in international revenues, imports were curtailed, but equilibrium in the balance of payments was not attained until 1962.[4] Additional problems included meeting the foreign debts incurred by the dictator.

Fiscal difficulties, along with political instability, a decline in oil prices, and a drop in iron production were hardly conducive to economic prosperity during the first three years of the Betancourt administration. The big construction industry came to a virtual standstill, as did expansion in the oil and iron industries. Business was depressed generally from 1959 to 1961.

The state of the union messages to Congress in early 1960, 1961, and 1962 painted uniformly gloomy economic pictures. Each year the President remarked how the recession was lasting longer than anticipated and that as a result the Government's development plans were falling behind schedule. During 1960 the Gross National Product rose only 1·4 per cent., in 1961 only 1·7 per cent.; thus per capita income, due to the annual population increase of more than 3 per cent. declined during both these years. Economic recuperation did not take place until 1962 when the Gross National Product rose 6 per cent. and

[4] A decree of 18 January 1964 terminated control and fixed a unified rate of Bs. 4.40 to the $ both for exports of petroleum and other minerals and for essential imports. For the proceeds of coffee and cacao exports the new rate was Bs. 4.485 to the $. The banks' free-market rate was now Bs. 4.50 (Bank of London & South America, *Fortnightly Review*, 8 Feb. 1964, suppl.).

per capita income 2·4 per cent. During 1963 the recovery continued; prices were stabilized; the flight of capital was reversed; international reserves rose to $750,000 million; the Gross National Product and per capita income continued to rise; domestic industry kept on growing, and business improved generally. However, about one-eighth of the labour force still remained without employment.

POLITICAL PROBLEMS

Serious as were the President's economic problems, they paled into insignificance beside the political problems he was compelled to face during his five years in office. In sharp contradistinction to his somewhat sectarian political attitude of the 1945–8 period, Betancourt in 1959 displayed a spirit of compromise and co-operation in his dealings with other political parties. Initially, in accordance with a pre-election pact, he set up a coalition Government which included leaders of the two other major parties, the Christian Democrats (COPEI) and the Republican Democratic Union (URD). Co-operation with other parties did not mean abandonment of the AD programme. However, Betancourt now sought to implement it more slowly and cautiously, using the methods of diplomacy and persuasion rather than trying to overwhelm the opposition with the majorities AD had in both houses of Congress.

These moderate tactics, however, soon brought the President into open conflict with the youth movement inside his own party. Already at the 1958 party convention, it was apparent there was an ideological conflict between the moderate, Old Guard party founders, led by Betancourt, Leoni, and Gonzalo Barrios, and the impatient Marxist-oriented university groups led by Domingo Alberto Rangel. The latter lost confidence in the Old Guard's evolutionary policies and preached revolution *á la* Castro as the only solution for Venezuela's social evils. Outvoted in the party convention, they bided their time until after Betancourt's inauguration, then launched increasingly bitter attacks against the prevailing moderation and the coalition government. Rangel and his associates fought openly against party president Leoni at the September 1959 AD convention. Following continued public criticism of the party's moderate position on such issues as Cuba, labour policy, and oil policy, the Old Guard leadership, unable to discipline the youth leaders, cashiered these 'Young Turks' (including fifteen members of the Chamber of Deputies) from the party in April 1960. This group, which represented a majority of the AD youth membership, promptly formed their own political organization called the Movement of the Revolutionary Left (MIR).

The MIR soon made common cause with Betancourt's other opposition, the Communist Party. The latter had been the only party excluded from the coalition. 'The Philosophy of Communism is not compatible with the development of Venezuela', Betancourt asserted. He repeatedly attacked the Communists in public and refused to have anything to do with a party whose members, he declared, were agents of Russian imperialism and whose methods were inimical to democratic processes.

Following the MIR-Old Guard schism, the governing coalition began to break down. When this was set up, the URD, led by Jovito Villalba, grumbled that it had received less than its fair share of offices and influence inside the coalition. It also began to criticize the administration for its overly moderate reform pace, its lack of sufficient sympathy for Castro's Cuba, and its subservience to Yankee imperialism. In November 1960 the URD withdrew from the coalition and six months later took up a position of uncompromising opposition to the Betancourt administration.

But the worst was still to come, for yet another schism rent Acción Democrática during 1961. This split was provoked by a middle-aged group, the youth of the 1945–8 period of AD rule, who tried to wrest control of the party from the Old Guard. This group, which assumed the label ARS (the initials of an advertising agency), had co-operated with the Old Guard against the MIR element, but following that schism became increasingly restless. ARS leaders, such as Raúl Ramos Jiménez and Ramón Quijada denounced the coalition Government and the excessive moderation of the agrarian programme, but the controversy was basically more personal than ideological. ARS leaders simply wanted to take over party leadership posts and ultimately the Presidency. The challenge was narrowly beaten back in the December 1961 party convention, whereupon ARS partisans resigned from the party and set up a rival political organization, which became known as AD-Opposition.

The ARS schism was truly a severe blow to AD. Many of the defectors were key union leaders and this threatened the party's long-standing alliance with organized labour and the peasantry. Worse still, ARS promptly joined forces with the URD, MIR, and Communist Party (PCV) opposition in Congress, and this opposition coalition during 1962 and 1963 obtained control of the Chamber of Deputies. The Government AD–COPEI coalition narrowly retained control of the Senate. Fortunately, nearly all the President's basic reform legislation had been enacted during the years 1959–61, and, in consequence, the Chamber of Deputies could do little but criticize, complain, and engage in obstructionist tactics while the administration pushed ahead with its manifold reform programmes.

The Marxist parties, however, the MIR and the PCV, did not confine themselves to legal opposition. At Betancourt's inauguration in Caracas, where the pro-rural President had received very little support, the PCV fomented a serious riot in protest against its exclusion from the coalition. During the remainder of 1959 it fished for support in the swelling ranks of the unemployed, inciting violence and mob-protest demonstrations against the Government.

During 1960 the PCV found valuable allies in terrorism and violence in the MIR and its University-student supporters. The extreme leftists were dominant at Central University. Imbued with a radicalism characteristic of Venezuelan youth, the students too were intolerant of political moderation; they idolized Castro; they felt their country exploited by United States capital in co-operation with an administration they believed ill-suited to Venezuela's urgent social needs. These students proved not only adept in the arts of rabble-rousing, sabotage, terrorism, and robbery, but they also succeeded in making use of the University's traditional autonomy to provide a sanctuary, a kind of political extra-territoriality, from which the extra-legal opponents of the administration might operate.

So serious did the PCV-MIR-student pro-Cuba rioting and violence become during the summer and fall of 1960, that the President in November of that year suspended constitutional guarantees. This move was understandably denounced by PCV and MIR Congressmen, and in April 1961 URD joined their demand for the restoration of constitutional guarantees. The President, however, pointing out that there was no let-up in extremist activities designed to incite violence and rebellion, refused; and Congress backed him. Following the ARS defection, however, the administration was in a less comfortable position, for during 1962 and 1963 the Chamber of Deputies began demanding an end to the administration's 'dictatorial' tactics. The authoritarian methods of the administration, said the opposition, were the very thing that provoked and intensified the violence.

Yet during early 1962 a temporary restoration of constitutional guarantees only seemed to give added license to terrorists. By the spring, several small guerrilla bands were operating in the West Andean states (under student

189

and Communist leadership), while bombings, robberies, bus burnings, and police assassinations continued to be the order of the day in Caracas. Such acts were abetted by the capital's juvenile delinquents. In May and June 1962, the Government uncovered unmistakable evidence of involvement by PCV and MIR party leaders in Marine Corps rebellions at Carúpano and Puerto Cabello. This, to Betancourt, was sufficient cause for 'suspending' the MIR and PCV parties until such time as the Supreme Court should decide whether they ought to be outlawed. The URD and ARS disagreed and reiterated their demands for restoration of constitutional guarantees.

The suspended parties promptly formed a determined terrorist organization called the Armed Forces of National Liberation (FALN) and stepped up the campaign to bring down the Betancourt Government. Apparently their aim was to provoke a military coup, following which they hoped to launch a violent social upheaval. FALN's hard core was small (perhaps less than a thousand), but their record was impressive. During 1962 they killed or wounded more than eighty policemen, burned seventy-five buses, robbed numerous business establishments, and performed repeated acts of sabotage in the oilfields. Their 1963 antics included the theft of paintings on loan from the Louvre, hijacking a freighter and an airliner, kidnapping a Spanish soccer player, and a United States military-mission officer, burning, bombing, and robbery of banks and business firms, plus the usual murders of policemen.

As the December elections approached, acts designed to provoke a military coup against the administration became even bolder. In September an attempt was made to assassinate the Defence Minister, and five National Guardsmen were murdered. These outrages prompted Betancourt, probably in anticipation of military demands, to order on 29 September the mass round-up and arrest of hundreds of leftist extremists. Simultaneously, the army came into the streets to combat the FALN. Charging that

MIR and PCV senators and deputies had used their congressional immunity to incite violence and rebellion, President Betancourt ordered them to be arrested and turned over to the military courts for trial. The ARS and the URD condemned the move. In this troubled, heated atmosphere, with the FALN threatening to shoot anyone who went to the polls, the presidential and congressional elections of 1 December 1963 were conducted.

BETANCOURT AND THE ARMED FORCES

One key reason why Betancourt was able to serve out his full term of office, the first popularly elected President in Venezuela's entire history to do so, was his success in dealing with the armed forces, traditionally the chief menace to constitutional government and democratic processes. The President's policy, from the very beginning, was to convince the military that he was sympathetic to their institutional needs and aspirations. In his frequent messages to the nation he rarely failed to compliment the armed forces for their apolitical, professional comportment and their loyalty and patriotism. Never forgetting that they always had the power to depose him, he approved, without question, liberal defence budgets, and frequently reiterated (and often exaggerated) the important role the military should be prepared to play in defending the country's borders and preserving internal order. The President rarely missed a military ceremony, was liberal with promotions, and promptly assumed his constitutional role of 'Commander-in-Chief of the National Armed Forces' when public order was threatened.

The armed forces' customary suspicion of civilian politicians, and especially reformers, was far from obliterated, but the President did much to heal the traditional breach between civilian and military elements. He tried to convince the military of the advantages to them of a democratic constitutional system and of the danger of annihilation of their institution by an aroused populace should they attempt to reimpose a Pérez Jiménez-type dictatorship. He made it unmistakably clear to the military that for them to intervene politically was to play directly into the hands of their worst enemies—the PCV and the MIR.

While the President's arguments were not always convincing, he was able to benefit from inter-service rivalry and competition. The army, from which a rightist threat was most dangerous, was in temporary disgrace because of the shame of its association with the Pérez Jiménez dictatorship. The navy, on the other hand, was in the ascendant. It was the hero of the 1958 revolution which toppled the dictatorship. Also, its new 5,000-man marine corps was resented by the infantry branch of the army. It was from the navy that a potential leftist threat loomed, for when Admiral Wolfgang Larrazábal, who had been supported by the Communists and the Caracas mobs in the 1958 elections, assumed a diplomatic post, his brother Admiral Carlos Larrazábal, and his brother-in-law, Admiral Sosa Ríos, assumed the top posts in the navy. The President attempted to steer a middle course between the embittered army and navy by favouring the air force, often at the expense of the other two. For example, Air Force Brigadier General Antonio Briceño Linares was Defence Minister during most of the Presidential term and another air force general was Chairman of the Joint Chiefs of Staff.

During his first three years of office, the military threat to the Government came principally from the rightist elements in the army, where rumours were rife during 1959 of violent officer-corps opposition to the Betancourt Government. Several minor plots were uncovered, and a number of suspected officers were dismissed. In April 1960 a retired air-force general, hoping for army support, launched an abortive invasion from Colombia. During 1961 cashiered officers of the Pérez Jiménez era attempted several coups. Involved in a May coup attempt was a former head of the National Guard. The following month other Pérez Jiménez officers seized the Barcelona army garrison in eastern Venezuela, but they were quickly put down by a combined assault by the three services.

The following year, 1962, the navy-leftist threat materialized in the form of uprisings by marine-corps battalions (in co-operation with the PCV and MIR) at Carúpano (in eastern Venezuela) in May and at Puerto Cabello in June. These uprisings were crushed, after considerable bloodshed, by joint army and air force assaults directed by the President himself from his command post in Caracas.

Throughout the remainder of his term, the President was able to avoid direct military pressures against his administration by taking prompt and stern measures against the leftist extremists whose terrorist actions were threatening a breakdown of law and order. But he refused to combat terror with terror. He argued that to act outside the law and the constitution would lead him down the path of dictatorship, a path he was determined not to follow. Retirements, transfers, and selective promotions were used to keep the more impatient officers in line, and even when it became necessary to take very drastic action against the leftist extremists, the President made every effort to operate strictly within the nation's legal and constitutional framework. His move to outlaw the PCV and MIR and his abrogation of congressional immunity for their deputies may have come partly in anticipation of military pressures to take such measures. These actions, the opposition charged, were the price the President was paying in order to ensure his own political survival.

FOREIGN AFFAIRS

In the realm of diplomacy, Venezuela had especially serious problems with two of her Caribbean neighbours. During the first half of his administration, the President's opponent was General Rafael Trujillo of the Dominican Republic; in the latter half it was Fidel Castro of Cuba.

The former gave support to the military rightists and the latter aided the leftist extremists in repeated attempts to destroy the Betancourt Government.

In retaliation against Trujillo, Venezuelan delegates on the Inter-American Peace Committee of the Organization of American States (OAS) brought formal charges against the dictatorship during 1959 and 1960 for flagrant violation of human rights. The result? The President only narrowly escaped assassination (he was burned severely by the bomb) at the hands of Trujillo's agents in Caracas on 24 June 1960. Thereupon, at Venezuela's instigation, the OAS members voted to sever diplomatic relations with the Dominican Republic. In January 1962, nine months after Trujillo was assassinated, Venezuela re-established diplomatic ties with Santo Domingo, but promptly severed them again in September 1963, following the overthrow of Juan Bosch's constitutional Government by the armed forces.

Inasmuch as Castro and Betancourt came to power in their respective countries about the same time, and inasmuch as both were avowed revolutionary reformers, the extremist, authoritarian techniques of the former inevitably invited comparison with the moderate, democratic methods of the latter. From the beginning, Betancourt's leftist opposition made no secret of the fact that it was working towards the establishment of a Castro-type régime in Venezuela, and by early 1960 it became apparent that Castro was reciprocating with both public and clandestine support to the PCV and MIR. In March 1960 the Venezuelan Government refused to attend the proposed Havana Conference of underdeveloped nations. In August it supported the OAS censure of Cuba for acceptance of Soviet military aid. Meanwhile, traditional economic ties dwindled to nothing as Venezuela approached self-sufficiency in domestic sugar production and Cuba began using Russian rather than Venezuelan oil in her refineries. The year 1961 was one of charges and countercharges about political interference culminating in the breaking off of diplomatic relations in November. Two months later Venezuela joined the majority at del Este, Uruguay, in expelling Cuba from thePunta OAS.

During the years 1962 and 1963 the Betancourt Government became convinced that Venezuela had been singled out by the Soviet Union and Cuba as the number one target in Latin America for the next Communist take-over. The actions of the PCV, the MIR, and the FALN, the violence, robberies, sabotage, and assassinations all pointed toward this conclusion. Concrete evidence of what had long been more than suspected, (a three-ton cache of small arms and ammunition from Cuba) was uncovered by the Government late in November 1963. Betancourt promptly took the matter before the OAS and called for 'joint definite action to finish with this bridgehead of Communism in America".[5]

Close ideological and economic ties tended to ensure that Betancourt's principal diplomatic relations would be with the United States. During 1958 relations had become temporarily strained when Caracas mobs attacked Vice-President Richard Nixon in a demonstration of their disapproval of the warm support previously afforded by the United States Government to the Pérez Jiménez régime. But once Betancourt took office, over-all relations with Washington were most cordial, for both régimes were in accord in their antagonism toward Communism and Cuba, and the Betancourt administration, with its impressive record of economic change, social reform, and democratic progress was proclaimed a model government under the Alliance for Progress programme. President John Kennedy visited Venezuela in December 1961, and in February 1963 Betancourt returned the visit.

There were some economic issues, nearly all of them centering on petroleum. The Venezuelan Government's arbitrary action in raising oil taxes in 1958 and its decision

[5] *New York Times*, 2 Dec. 1963.

in 1959 to enter the oil business caused considerable consternation among United States (as well as British and Dutch) investors. On the other hand, Venezuelans were greatly concerned by the United States Government's restricting of oil imports in 1959. During 1962 a further threat to the market for Venezuelan oil loomed up when the United States exempted from her quota system overland shipments of oil from Canada and Mexico. Venezuela demanded to be put on an equal footing with these two countries.

Throughout Betancourt's five years in office, his Government was involved with the United States over the person of the exiled dictator, Pérez Jiménez. Upon taking power, the administration protested against his residence in Miami. In August 1959 it brought formal charges against him for murder and peculation, and requested the United States to extradite him under the terms of the 1922 United States–Venezuela extradition treaty. For the next four years, the case wound its way through the United States courts, and in August 1963 Pérez Jiménez was extradited to his homeland to face trial on charges of 'peculation, extortion, corruption of officials, and abuse of authority'.

The Pérez Jiménez extradition case was part of an international campaign conducted by the Betancourt Government's diplomats and jurists to set up a kind of world-wide extradition accord under which fleeing government officials who had enriched themselves with public monies would be sent back, along with their stolen goods, to their native lands for trial.

In addition, the Betancourt administration embarked on a hemisphere-wide campaign against the use of force to overturn constitutional Governments. While it repeatedly urged the OAS to take collective action, it took unilateral action in severing relations with all régimes resulting from military coups—with Argentina in March 1962, Peru in July 1962, Guatemala in March 1963, Ecuador in July

1963, the Dominican Republic in September 1963, and Honduras in October 1963. At the very end of his term, the President had the satisfaction of seeing the heretofore reluctant OAS at least agree to discuss possible collective measures to strengthen democracy in Latin America.

THE 1963 ELECTIONS

The presidential and congressional elections of 1 December 1963 provided the Venezuelan people with the opportunity to render judgment upon the Government and its programmes. The AD-COPEI coalition underwent severe strain over the question of who was to succeed President Rómulo Betancourt. Although he declared, early in 1963, that there was no heir apparent and that he would scrupulously refrain from designating one, it was clear that the President's overwhelming prestige in the AD party would result in the nomination of the candidate most acceptable to his wishes. This was party president Raúl Leoni, a man closely and continuously associated with Betancourt for thirty-five years. Leoni too was of the so-called 'generation of 1928', a student protest leader against the Gómez dictatorship. He accompanied Betancourt into exile, returned with him in 1936 to begin organizing what eventually became the Acción Democrática Party, became Betancourt's Labour Minister in 1945–8, returned from exile following the fall of Pérez Jiménez to manage the 1959 presidential campaign of Betancourt, and succeeded him in the party presidency during the years 1959 to 1963.

AD's selection of Leoni was a grave disappointment to COPEI. For five years of loyal co-operation with AD in the governing coalition, its leaders expected political reward in the form of a 'coalition candidate', this time to be selected from COPEI. When AD, without consultation, named Leoni, COPEI named its party president Rafael Caldera to oppose him.

The parties of the anti-government coalition were likewise unable to agree on a single candidate. Admiral Wolf-gang Larrazábal, who ran second to Betancourt in 1958, re-entered the campaign, but this time URD nominated party president Jovito Villalba, thus leaving the admiral bereft of organized party support. AD-Opposition (ARS) also nominated its party leader, Raúl Ramos Jiménez, and this left Arturo Uslar Pietri, an independent aspirant and a former minister in the Government of General Medina (1941–5), without significant party backing. A seventh candidate, also an independent, was far-rightist Germán Borregales. The PCV and MIR remained under 'suspension' through the 1963 election period.

The candidates deriving from the governing coalition, Leoni and Caldera, ran on the Government's record. Leoni's programme was one of continuity, to maintain intact the political policies of Betancourt (coalition government, democratic processes, anti-Communism, international co-operation) and to push towards completion of his social and economic programmes (agrarian reform, industrialization, more housing, hospitals, roads and schools, and reduction of unemployment and illiteracy). The scope and pace of Caldera's proposed programmes were quite similar to Leoni's; he argued that he could do the job better.

The five other candidates, however, assailed the Betancourt record in no uncertain terms. They proclaimed the agrarian-reform programme an utter failure, the housing programme woefully inadequate, the economic programme a near disaster, and foreign policy a sell-out to Yankee imperialism. The President's long suspension of constitutional guarantees was declared both illegal and unnecessary, a crude device to screen his ineptitude for dealing with his political opponents and curbing violence by legal means. Larrazábal, Ramos Jiménez, and Villalba called for a drastic speed-up in the pace of social reform, intensified economic nationalism, and a more independent foreign-policy line.

The popular mandate rendered on 1 December 1963 was as follows:

For President	Votes	Per cent.
Leoni (AD)	957,699	33
Caldera (COPEI)	589,372	20
Uslar Pietri (IPFN)	551,120	19
Villalba (URD)	469,240	16
Larrazábal (FDP)	275,304	10
Ramos Jiménez (ARS)	66,837	2
Borregales	9,324	—

For Congress	Senate	Chamber of Deputies
AD	21	64
COPEI	9	40
URD	6	27
IPFN	3	19
FDP	3	14
ARS	—	1

This was a victory, though not an overwhelming one, for the governing coalition, a vote for moderate evolutionary reform policies; it was a rejection of both rightist and leftist extremism, especially the latter. The AD–COPEI coalition not only increased its majority in the Senate but also regained control of the Chamber of Deputies. In the Presidential race, as in 1958, it was the vote from the countryside that spelled victory for the AD candidate. Uslar Pietri won in Caracas. The most impressive political gains, however, were made by COPEI. Caldera's vote, and that of his party, was up 7 per cent. over 1958, while that of AD had declined (due to MIR and ARS defections) by more than double this amount, all of which meant that the Christian Democrats were going to exercise a still more powerful voice in national politics.

As President Betancourt neared the end of his term of office and prepared to turn over the reins of power to his duly elected successor, he was asked, 'Of what achievements of your term as President are you most proud?' He replied that, 'The most important thing achieved by my government is to show that in a country like Venezuela, where there have been so many dictators, a democratic and representative régime can function.'[6] On 11 March 1964 Raúl Leoni was inaugurated President of Venezuela for the constitutional term of office 1964–9.

[6] *New York Times*, 17 Oct. 1963.

BIBLIOGRAPHY

BIBLIOGRAPHICAL AIDS

Anuario bibliográfico venezolano. Caracas, 1944.

Clagett, Helen L. *A Guide to the Law and Legal Literature of Venezuela.* Washington, Lib. of Congress, 1947.

Grases, Pedro. *Temas de bibliografía y cultura venezolanas.* Buenos Aires, 1953.

García Chuecos, Hector. *Catálogo de documentos referentes a historia de Venezuela y de América existentes en el Archivo Nacional de Washington.* Caracas, 1950.

Humphreys, R. A. *Latin American History; a Guide to the Literature in English.* London, Oxford U.P. for RIIA., 1958.

Neuberger, Otto, *A Guide to the Official Publications of the other American Republics. XIX: Venezuela.* Washington, Lib. of Congress, 1948.

Resumen cronológico de las leyes y decretos del crédito público de Venezuela, desde el año 1826. Caracas, 1873.

Sánchez, Manuel Segundo. *Bibliografía venezolanista: Contribución al conocimiento de los libros extranjeros relativos a Venezuela y sus grandes hombres.* Caracas, 1914.

United States Library of Congress. *List of writings on the Venezuela Case, 1902–1903.* Washington, 1908.

GENERAL

Briceño, Olga. *Cocks and Bulls in Caracas.* Boston, Houghton Mifflin, 1945.

Dalton, L. C. *Venezuela.* London, 1912.

Fergusson, Erna. *Venezuela.* New York, Knopf, 1939.

Jones Parra, Juan. *Pocket Atlas of Venezuela.* Caracas, Miangolarra Hnos., 1957.

Kirchhoff, Herbert. *Venezuela.* Buenos Aires, Kraft, 1956.

Royal Institute of International Affairs. *Venezuela; a Brief Political and Economic Survey.* London, 1958.

Uslar Pietri, Arturo. *De Una a otra Venezuela.* Caracas, 1950.

Veloz Goiticoa, N. *Venezuela—1924.* Caracas, Lit. y Tip. del Comercio, 1924.

Bibliography

Venezuela, Min. de Relaciones Exteriores. *Venezuela en 1956.* Caracas, 1957.

Ward, Edward. *The New El Dorado: Venezuela.* London, Hale, 1957.

Wohlrabe, Raymond A. *The Land and People of Venezuela.* Philadelphia, Lippincott, 1959.

THE LAND

Beebe, Charles William. *High Jungle.* New York, Duell, Sloan & Pierce, 1949.

Bingham, Hiram. *The Journal of an Expedition Across Venezuela and Colombia, 1906–1907.* New Haven, Yale U.P., 1909.

Bucher, Walter H. *Geologic Structure and Organic History of Venezuela.* New York, 1952.

Codazzi, Giovanni B. A. *Resumen de la geografía de Venezuela.* Paris, Fournier, 1841.

Cova, Jesús Antonio. *Geografía física y política de Venezuela.* Caracas, Elite, 1936.

Humboldt, Alexander von. *Personal Narrative of Travels to the Equinoctial Regions of the New Continent during the years 1799–1804,* trans. by Helen Maria Williams. London, 1814–29. 7 vols.

Liddle, Ralph A. *Geology of Venezuela and Trinidad,* 2nd ed. Ithaca, N.Y., 1946.

MacDonald, Norman. *The Orchid Hunters; a Jungle Adventure.* New York, Farrar & Rinehart, 1939.

Nesbitt, Ludovico. *Desolate Marches; Travels in the Orinoco Llanos of Venezuela.* New York, Harcourt, Brace, 1936.

Russell, William R. *The Bolivar Countries: Colombia, Ecuador, Venezuela.* New York, Coward-McCann, 1949.

Sievers, William. *Geografía de Ecuador, Colombia y Venezuela,* trans. from the German by Carlos de Salas. Barcelona, Edit. Labor, 1931.

Vila, Marco Aurelio. *Geografía de Venezuela,* 3rd ed. Caracas, Fundación Eugenio Mendoza, 1956.

Zuloaga, Guillermo. *A Geographical Glimpse of Venezuela.* Caracas, Cromotip, 1957.

THE PEOPLE

Acosta Saignes, Miguel. *Estudios de etnología antigua de Venezuela.* Caracas, 1954.

Bibliography

Arcaya, Pedro Manual. *Estudios de sociología venezolana*. Caracas, Cecilio Acosta, 1941.

Bengoa y Lecanda, Jose María. *Medicina social en el medio rural venezolana*. Caracas, Grafolit, 1946.

International Labour Office. *Freedom of Association and Conditions of Work in Venezuela*. Geneva, 1950.

Siso, Carlos. *La Formación del pueblo venezolano*. New York, Horizon House, 1941.

Venezuela, Consejo de Bienestar Rural. *Problemas económicos y sociales de los Andes venezolanos*. Caracas, 1955-6. 2 vols.

—— Dirección Gen. de Estadística. *Séptimo censo nacional de población levantado el 7 de diciembre de 1941*. Caracas, 1944.

—— Min. de Fomento. *IX censo de población*. Caracas, 1962.

—— Oficina Central del Censo Nacional. *Octavo censo general de población, 26 de noviembre de 1950*. Caracas, 1954.

HISTORY

Baralt, Rafael María. *Resumen de la historia de Venezuela*. Paris, Desclée, de Brouwer, 1939.

García Chuecos, Héctor. *Estudios de historia colonial venezolana*. Caracas, Tipografía Americana, 1937-8. 2 vols.

Gil Fortoul, José. *Historia constitucional de Venezuela*. 4th ed. Caracas, 1953-5. 3 vols.

Gonzalez Guinán, Francisco. *Historia contemporaria de Venezuela*. Caracas, 1909-11. 10 vols.

Hasbrouck, Alfred. *Foreign Legionaries in the Liberation of Spanish South America*. New York, Columbia U.P., 1928.

Hussey, Roland D. *The Caracas Company, 1728-1784*. London, Oxford U.P., 1934.

Lieuwen, Edwin. *Petroleum in Venezuela; a History*. Berkeley, California U.P., 1954. (Univ. of Calif. Publications in History, xlvi.)

López Contreras, Eleazar. *Páginas para la historia militar de Venezuela*. Caracas, 1945.

Marsland, William D. *Venezuela through its History*. New York, Crowell, 1954.

Masur, Gerhard. *Simón Bolívar*. Albuquerque, New Mexico U.P., 1948.

Oviedo y Baños, José de. *Historia de la conquista y población de la provincia de Venezuela*. Madrid, L. Navarro, 1885.

Bibliography

Robertson, W. A. *The Life of Miranda*. Chapel Hill, North Carolina U.P., 1929. 2 vols.

Siso Martínez, J. M. *Historia de Venezuela*. Mexico, Servicio Impreso, 1954.

Watters, Mary. *A History of the Church in Venezuela*. Chapel Hill, North Carolina U.P., 1933.

POLITICS

Arcaya, Pedro Manuel. *Venezuela y su actual régimen*. Baltimore, 1935.

Betancourt, Rómulo. *Rómulo Betancourt: pensamiento y acción*. Mexico, 1951.

—— *Venezuela: política y petróleo*. Mexico, Fondo de Cultura Económica, 1956.

Gabaldón Márquez, Joaquín. *Archivos de una inquietud venezolana*. Caracas, 1955.

Gil, Pío. *El Cabito*. Caracas, 1936.

Graham, Robbert, B. C. *José Antonio Páez*. Philadelphia, Macrae, Smith, 1929.

Lavin, John. *A Halo for Gómez*. New York, Pageant, 1954.

López Contreras, Eleazar. *El Triunfo de la verdad*. Mexico, Edición Genio Latero, 1949.

Lugo, Francisco A. *Pérez Jiménez; fuerza creadora*. 2nd ed. Caracas, Impr. Nacional, 1954.

Páez, José Antonio. *Autobiografía del General José Antonio Páez*. New York, Hallet & Breen, 1867.

Pérez Jiménez, Marcos. *Pensamiento político del Presidente de Venezuela*. Caracas, Impr. Nacional, 1954.

Rondón Márquez, Rafael Angel. *Guzmán Blanco, 'el autócrata civilizador'*. 2nd ed. Madrid, Garcia Vicente, 1952.

Rourke, Thomas. *Gómez; Tyrant of the Andes*. New York, Morrow, 1941.

Tarnói, Ladislao. *El nuevo ideal nacional de Venezuela; vida y obra de Marcos Pérez Jiménez*. Madrid, Ediciones Verdad, 1954.

Umaña Bernal, José. *Testimonios de la revolución en Venezuela*. Caracas, 1958.

Vallenilla Lanz, Laureano. *Cesarismo democrático*. 3rd ed. Caracas, Garrido, 1952.

Wise, George S. *Caudillo; a Portrait of Antonio Guzmán Blanco*. New York, Colombia U.P., 1951.

Bibliography

THE ECONOMY

Arcila Farías, Eduardo. *Economía colonial de Venezuela*. Mexico, Fondo de Cultura Económica, 1946.

Arráiz, Antonio. *Geografía económica de Venezuela*. Caracas, Cultural Venezolana, 1956.

Banco Central de Venezuela. *Boletín*. Caracas, 1941–
—— *Memoria*. Caracas, 1941– .

Econometric Specialists, Inc. *United States Trade with Venezuela*. New York, 1954.

Egaña, Manuel R. *Tres décadas de producción petrolera*. Caracas, 1947.

Fernández y Fernández, Ramón. *Reforma agraria en Venezuela*. Caracas, 1948.

Great Britain, Dept. of Overseas Trade. *Report on the Economic and Commercial Conditions of Venezuela*. London, 1921–35.

Inter-American Development Commission. *The Industries of Venezuela*. Washington, 1948.

International Bank for Reconstruction and Development. *The Economic Development of Venezuela*. Baltimore, Johns Hopkins Press for IBRD, 1961.

Jankus, Alfred P. *Venezuela; Land of Opportunity*. New York, Pageant, 1956.

León, Ramón David. *De Agro-pecuario a petróleo*. Caracas, 1944.

Luzardo, Rodolfo. *Venezuela; Business and Finances*. Englewood Cliffs, N.J., Prentice-Hall, 1957.

Moll, Roberto. *Lecciones de economía venezolana*. Caracas, Litografía del Comercio, 1944.

Pogue, Joseph E. *Oil in Venezuela*. New York, Chase National Bank, 1949.

Rangel, Domingo Alberto. *La Industrialización de Venezuela*. Caracas, Pensamienta Viva, 1958.

U.S. Bureau of Foreign and Domestic Commerce. *Investment in Venezuela*. Washington, 1953.

—— —— *Venezuela: a Commercial and Industrial Handbook*. Washington, 1922.

U.S. Tariff Commission. *Mining and Manufacturing in Venezuela*. Washington, 1949.

Uslar Pietri, Arturo. *Sumario de economía venezolana*. 2nd ed. Caracas, 1958.

Bibliography

Venezuela, Corporación de Fomento. *Cuadernos de información de fomento.* Caracas, 1949– .

―― Dirección Gen de Estadística. *Anuario Estadístico de Venezuela.* Caracas, 1877– .

―― ―― *Boletín mensual de estadística.* Caracas, 1947– .

―― ―― *Censos industrial, comercial y empresas que prestan servicios, 1936.* Caracas, 1937–41. 23 vols.

―― Min. de Agricultura y Cría. *Censo agrícola y pecuario.* Caracas, 1941.

―― Min. de Minas y Hidrocarburos. *Anuario petróleo y minero de Venezuela.* Caracas, 1955– .

―― Min. de Relaciónes Exteriores. *Boletín comercial y industrial.* Caracas, 1920– .

INTERNATIONAL RELATIONS

Cleveland, Grover. *The Venezuelan Boundary Controversy.* N.J., Princeton U.P., 1913.

Parra, Francisco J. *Doctrinas de la cancillería venezolana.* New York, Las Americas, 1952. 2 vols.

Plaza, Eduardo R. *La Contribución de Venezuela al Pan Americanismo durante el periodo 1939–1943.* Caracas, 1945.

Thurber, Orray E. *The Venezuelan Question; Castro and the Asphalt Trust.* New York, 1947.

U.S.A., Commission to Investigate and Report on the True Divisional Line Between Venezuela and British Guiana. *Report and Accompanying Papers.* Washington, 1896–7. 8 vols.

―― Dept. of State. *Correspondence Relating to Wrongs Done to American Citizens by the Government of Venezuela.* Washington, 1908.

Venezuela. *Historia oficial de la discusión entre Venezuela y la Gran Bretaña sobre sus límites en la Guayana.* New York, Weiss, 1896.

―― Min. de Relaciones Exteriores. *Boletín.* Caracas, 1909– .

―― ―― *El Libro amarillo.* Caracas, 1894– .

INDEX

Index

209

Index

Monagas, José Gregorio, 37
Monagas, José Tadeo, 36–7, 39
Movement of the Revolutionary Left (MIR), 187 ff., 198 f.

National Electrification Plan, 130–1
National Railways Autonomous Institute, 148
National security police, 92, 94–5, 99
Naval Blockade of 1902–3, 44, 170
Negroes, 12, 26–27
New Granada, Viceroyalty of, 23

Ocaña, Convention of, 32
Oil, *see* Petroleum
Ojeda, Alonso de, 21
OPEC, 184
Organization of American States, 194 ff.
Orinoco: river, 1–3; delta, 2, 4
Orinoco Mining Co., *see* United States Steel Corp.
ORVE, 52, 54, 56, 64

Páez, José Antonio, 31–4, 63
Pan American Highway, 149–50
Pan Americanism, 173–4
Paraguaná peninsula, 4
Pardos, 26, 28–31
Patriotic Junta, 101–2
Patriotic Military Union (UPM), 69–70
PCV, *see* Communism
PDN, 56
PDV, 61–2, 67–8, 72
Pearl fishing, 22
Pérez Alfonso, Juan Pablo, 184
Pérez Jiménez, Marcos: early career, 89–90; political oppression, 91–3; education policy, 93–4, 97; press censorship, 94; character, 94; governing philosophy, 95–6; economic policy, 97; extravagance, 97–8; peculation, 98; opposition to, 98–101; exile, 102; deficit financing, 143; railway development plan, 148; foreign policy, 175–6; extradition of, 196
Petroleum, 2, 4, 7–8
Petroleum industry, 106, 108–14, 183–4, 195–6; early development of, 47–8; legislation, 47–8, 55, 58–9, 183; labour troubles, 52–4;

opening of *llanos*, 55; and Second World War, 58–9; and AD, 76–9; and Pérez Jiménez, 93, 96; taxes, 103, 112–13, 145, 196; production, 109, 111; refining, 111; exports, 111; 135 ff.,' reserves 111–12; concessions, 112; marketing, 112–13; profits, 113; investment, 113, 132; nationalization question, 113–14; and balance of payments, 139–40; pipelines, 150; and socio-economic change, 153–4; Anglo American rivalry in, 171–2; collective contracts, 181
Physiography, 1–8
Political parties, 162–3
Population, 10–11, 13, 179, 185
Presidential powers, 163
Protestantism, 20
Public finance, 141–6, 184–5
Puerto Cabello, 2–3
Puerto la Cruz, 3–4, 147, 150
Puerto Ordaz, 3, 115, 147 f.
Punta Cardón, 3, 111
Punta de Araya, 4

Race, 12
Railways, 147–9
Rainfall, 117–18
Rangel, Domingo Alberto, 186 f.
Real Compañía Guipuzcoana, *see* Caracas Company
Regionalism, 23–4, 32–3, 39, 43–4
Religion, *see* Church
Republican Democratic Union, *see* URD
Revolution: (1810), 28; (1858), 37; (1868), 40; (1902–3), 44; (1945), 63–70, 153–4; (1948), 85–9, 155; (1958,) 98–102
Río de Oro, 165–6
Roads, 149–50
Rockefeller, Nelson, 134
Royal Dutch-Shell, 110–11, 132

Salt, 117
San Tomé de Guayana, 183
Santander, Francisco de Paula, 32
Santo Domingo, Audiencia of, 23
Schomburgk line, 167–8
Scruggs, William, 167
'Sembrar el petróleo', 54
Shell, *see* Royal Dutch-Shell
Shipping, 147
Sierra de Perijá, 1–2, 4, 6, 17

210

Set by
The Broadwater Press
Welwyn Garden City
and
reprinted lithographically by
Latimer Trend & Co. Ltd.
Whitstable